Computational Frameworks

Computational Frameworks

Systems, Models and Applications

Edited by

Mamadou Kaba Traoré

ELSEVIER

First published 2017 in Great Britain and the United States by ISTE Press Ltd and Elsevier Ltd

ISTE Press Ltd
27-37 St George's Road
London SW19 4EU
UK

www.iste.co.uk

Elsevier Ltd
The Boulevard, Langford Lane
Kidlington, Oxford, OX5 1GB
UK

www.elsevier.com

Notices

Knowledge and best practice in this field are constantly changing. As new research and experience broaden our understanding, changes in research methods, professional practices, or medical treatment may become necessary.

Practitioners and researchers must always rely on their own experience and knowledge in evaluating and using any information, methods, compounds, or experiments described herein. In using such information or methods they should be mindful of their own safety and the safety of others, including parties for whom they have a professional responsibility.

To the fullest extent of the law, neither the Publisher nor the authors, contributors, or editors, assume any liability for any injury and/or damage to persons or property as a matter of products liability, negligence or otherwise, or from any use or operation of any methods, products, instructions, or ideas contained in the material herein.

For information on all our publications visit our website at http://store.elsevier.com/

British Library Cataloguing-in-Publication Data
A CIP record for this book is available from the British Library
Library of Congress Cataloging in Publication Data
A catalog record for this book is available from the Library of Congress
ISBN 978-1-78548-256-4

Printed and bound in the UK and US

Contents

**Chapter 2. Multidisciplinary, Interdisciplinary
and Transdisciplinary Federations
in Support of New Medical Simulation
Concepts: Harmonics for the Music of Life**   47
Andreas TOLK

**Chapter 3. Heterogeneous Computing:
An Emerging Paradigm of Embedded Systems Design**   61
Abderazak BEN ABDALLAH

Introduction

Introduction to Computational Frameworks: From Heterogeneity Challenge to Integrative Levels of Organization

The idea for this volume started at AUSTECH 2015, the first international multiconference in Technology of the African University of Science and Technology (AUST). We had organized it in October 12–14 2015, on the AUST campus in Abuja, Nigeria. AUSTECH 2015 focused on current developments in engineering technologies, and their scientific and industrial applications for development in sub-Saharan Africa. It hosted three symposia, each of them reflecting one of the core technological areas developed at AUST. Among them was the Computer Science Symposium (CSS), a platform to explore and facilitate the dissemination of the most recent advancements in the theories, technologies and applications of computational systems for development (with special emphasis on sub-Saharan Africa).

Computational Science and Engineering (CSE) is core to all engineering sciences. As a result, computational systems are seeing an explosion growth of services to all user domains worldwide: public or private, military or governmental, educational or industry, healthcare or finance and science or entertainment. Beyond their diversity, there is a unity of concerns, which can

Introduction written by Mamadou Kaba TRAORÉ.

be expressed through some key research questions. The use of computational technologies (e.g. high performance clusters, Big Data, databases and information systems, integrated and embedded hardware/software components, smart devices, mobile and pervasive networks, cyber physical systems, etc.) requires theoretical, methodological, technical, scaling and many other important issues to be studied, monitored and predicted in order to save costs and time and to add value to social capital.

CSS in AUSTECH 2015 brought together world-class researchers and students to share and discuss current challenges faced in the pursuit of advancing focused knowledge. It quickly appeared from the contributions that trends and key challenges can be seen from the perspective of computational frameworks. The quality of the presentations and the richness of exchanges led us to select four major contributions by well-recognized researchers to be chapters in a pioneering volume on CSE. It is unique in that it presents the views on computational systems, models and applications under one holistic scope. With such a very restrictive and highly selective set of contributions, this handbook aims at providing an overview in very advanced theoretical, methodological, technical and cognitive perspectives in the domain, while bridging the gap between frontline research and practical efforts.

I.1. Computational science and the challenge of heterogeneity

CSE is a relatively new discipline, commonly heralded as the third mode of discovery (next to theory and experimentation) [ODE 14, RAY 11]. Computational science is often described as fusing numerical methods (with a special focus on Modeling & Simulation (M&S)), computer systems (software and hardware, with a special focus on High Performance Computing) and information science (with a special focus on data management). Today, it is an essential component of modern research in different areas (computational physics, computational biology, computational chemistry, etc.) where it often bridges computer science, mathematics and domain-specific knowledge. It calls for the use of some computational approach that may also require the design of the supporting computational system or the use of an existing one. This is where computational frameworks come into play.

In all forms of CSE, there is a common barrier to the design and use of computational systems, which we call the heterogeneity challenge. Indeed, computational approaches are confronted to a universal complexity due to the need to integrate heterogeneous components into a homogeneous whole (i.e. the framework). Such heterogeneity can take at least one of the following forms:

– disparity of abstractions (often referred to as multiabstraction or multilevel) [BEN 98];

– diversity of details (often referred to as multiresolution) [DAV 93];

– variety of scales (often referred to as multiscale) [TAO 09];

– multiplicity of perspectives (often referred to as multiview or multiperspective) [REI 14];

– distribution of geographic locations (often referred to as multisite) [YAN 08].

As a way to draw attention how difficult this challenge is, the literature often resorts to the use of the prefix "multi". Terms like "multiphysics", "multiobjective" or "multiparadigm" are generalizations (and sometimes accumulations) of these forms of heterogeneity and their underlying complexity. From the literature, we can also derive the following four key requirements to overcome this barrier:

– a system-theoretic approach is needed for a deep and structured understanding of the phenomena involved. Bernard Zeigler has established a foundational system-theoretical framework suitable for systems analysis and design [ZEI 76, ZEI 84, ZEI 00]. In Chapter 1 of this volume, he explores, beyond the frontiers of individual system design, how to efficiently integrate them, leading to the design of System of Systems (SoSs). While a classic system design results in the building of a component that has its operational and managerial independence, the design of a cluster of such components (that, in addition, can be geographically distributed) addresses the evolutionary development issue, i.e. the emergence of functionalities that none of the component can (or was designed to) solve alone. Such emergence can be positive (i.e. desired) or negative (i.e. not wished). The concept of pathways is introduced to allow distributed individual-based tracking and to coordinate individual systems toward SoSs capable of completing specific desired goals/subgoals;

– a holistic approach is necessary for a sound cognitive management of the system or the SoS identified. That is what Andreas Tolk highlights in Chapter 2. In the same way that, technical integration is needed for SoSs, there is a parallel effort to do for the cognitive integration of multiple disciplines, with three levels of alignment: multidisciplinarity, interdisicplinarity and transdisciplinarity. The chapter shows how proper data concepts have to be semantically aligned and processes be synchronized. This is formalized in a Conceptual Interoperability Model;

– validity is always a critical (and often non-trivial) issue. David Hill and colleagues show in Chapter 4 that a common pitfall to all computational approaches is numerical reproducibility, i.e. the obtention from one environment to the other of the same execution results for a given computational experiment. This chapter discusses sources of non-reproducibility, specifically in the sensitive context of high-performance simulation, and makes recommendations to achieve a sound scientific validity;

– it is increasingly compulsory to use performant infrastructures to support computations as they are getting heavier with new areas and demands of CSE. Abderazak Ben Abdallah points out in Chapter 3 that conventional single-core-based designs are no longer suitable to satisfy high-performance and low-power consumption demands in new embedded applications. Designers, thus, turn toward the very hard task of integrating multiple cores on a single chip. The chapter explores alternatives to achieve such goal and examines their pros and cons.

Computational frameworks are a systematic and assessable way to answer the heterogeneity challenge. Here, we suggest four integrative levels of organization where computational frameworks can address each of the above-mentioned requirements.

I.2. Computational frameworks and the integrative levels of organization

Surprisingly, despite its wide use in the literature, the notion of "computational framework" has no specific and commonly agreed definition, while numerous definitions can be found for terms such as "framework" (https://en.wikipedia.org/wiki/Framework), "software framework" [GAC 03], "architecture framework" [HIL 04] and many others. Here, we try to provide working definitions, as we claim the term of "computational framework" is used to express various levels of understanding of one same general concept, and that those levels can be structured in a four-layer hierarchy.

As presented in Figure I.1, a computational framework can relate to:

– computational (hardware) systems, i.e. platforms designed to serve as computing systems. This ranges from original computer architectures to computer networks and high-performance architectures. This is the perspective of Chapter 3;

– computational (software) programs, where the basic concerns are modeling and programming. Chapter 4 can be seen from that perspective, with a focus on software's impact on reproducibility;

– computational theories elaborated for problem solving. This ranges from numerical approaches (numerical analysis, operations research, etc.) and logic to artificial intelligence and M&S. Chapter 1 can be placed in this perspective;

– computational applications (i.e. domain-specific methodologies, computations and general results). Chapter 2 can be seen from that perspective, with a generic discourse on multidisciplinary, interdisciplinary and transdisciplinary concepts and illustrations in the specific context of medical simulation;

– a combination of any 2, 3 or 4 or the formers. Sets in Figure I.1 are arranged such that the following are possible: (1)+(2), (1)+(3), (1)+(4), (1)+(2)+(3), (1)+(2)+(4), (1)+(3)+(4) and (1)+(2)+(3)+(4). This suggests that, at one hand, although frameworks can be defined and limited to each set, the ultimate aim of a computational system is to run on top of a given execution platform. On the other hand, when a computational system is associated with any component of any other set, the result is a computational system (e.g. a computational program running on top of a computational hardware system forms with the latter a computational system). Therefore, all associations involving level (1) are meaningful in that the core of the resulting system may be just a hardware system, a software system on top of a hardware system, a theory implemented in a software and running on a hardware, etc.

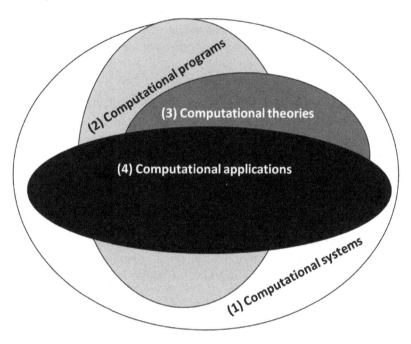

Figure I.1. *Computational systems components*

We propose the following working definitions:

DEFINITION 1.– A computational framework is a set of concepts, properties, rules and tools that can be of a theoretical, methodological, technical or technological nature, which are glued in a normative architecture, to ease and possibly automate the problem-solving process partly or entirely.

DEFINITION 2.– CSE deals with the development and application of computational frameworks to solve complex problems.

What Figure I.1 suggests in an intuitive way is made explicit in Figure I.2, where we show the integrative nature of the organization in which computational frameworks can be formalized.

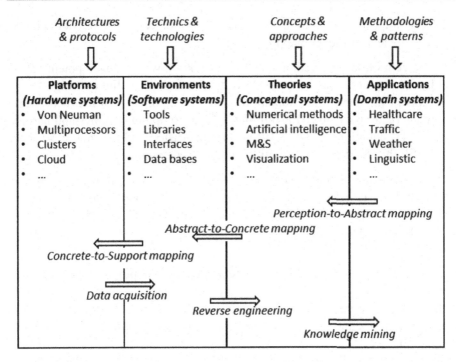

Figure I.2. *Integrative levels of organization for computational frameworks*

Computational frameworks can be defined at a:

– applications level, as in [CHA 13] for healthcare, [ALV 10] for civil engineering, [FLA 10] for metabolic networks, [ONE 11] for dramatic art and many others;

– theories level, as in [DOR 02] for geometry, [GAS 09] for nonlinear algebra, [ZEI 76] for discrete event simulation and many others;

– (software) environments level, as in [OMG 01] for distributed computing, [GAM 95] for object-oriented design, [STE 09] for Java code synthesis and many others;

– (hardware) platforms level, as in [ANG 06] for the design of multiprocessors on-chip, [PAT 01] for dynamic optimization of hardware systems, [FLE 13] for code acceleration on homogeneous multicores and many others.

Very importantly, computational frameworks can also be defined to address the level-to-level mapping issue, i.e.:

– perception-to-abstraction mapping, which allows the development of an application framework on top of a theoretical one, linking high-level concepts of the application domain to lower level concepts of the theoretical approach (examples are [BER 00] that bridges computer graphics and partial differential equations, [SOC 98] that bridges vision and geometric algebra and [LEE 99] that bridges network security and data mining);

– abstract-to-concrete mapping, which allows the translation of a theoretical framework's elements into their implementation counterparts (examples are [PUE 99] in interface development, [ATK 03] in model-driven system design and numerous computer-aided software engineering tools [FUG 93]);

– concrete-to-support mapping, which allows the deployment of software components onto hardware hosts (examples are the MPI framework [MPI 94] for distributed programming with general languages through message interfacing, and [FER 98] for parallel programming with Java language).

Similarly, some computational frameworks are defined to reverse this level-to-level stream, therefore using the lower level information to build the higher level. That is the case for:

– data acquisition frameworks, which go from platforms (generally an ecosystem of devices) to databases [VIL 13, CED 12, MER 13];

– reverse engineering frameworks, which go from codes to conceptual representations [BRU 14, ROY 08];

– knowledge mining frameworks, which enrich application knowledge with properties discovered/established at the theoretical level [PAL 12, VAN 05, FAY 96].

More importantly, advanced frameworks aggregate several levels and level-to-level mappings. For example, the Common Component Architecture is a standard software architecture allowing plug-and-play composition of scientific applications [RAY 11]. The High-Level Architecture (HLA) framework combines M&S theoretical framework with distributed computing environment framework [FUJ 98]. Lee et al. [LEE 03] extend the HLA framework to Discrete Event System Specification theoretical framework, on the one hand, and to the transportation application framework, on the other hand. Smarsly *et al.* [SMA 13] combine data acquisition (reverse process) and abstract-to-concrete mapping (numerical methods). Cui and Franchetti [CUI 12] cover the four integrative levels, bridging distribution systems application with high-performance computing through Monte Carlo simulation and a MATLAB-based solver.

I.3. Reading the volume

Few books are specifically devoted to computational frameworks. This volume will probably be one of the firsts to do so in a way that shows the interdisciplinary essence of this area and how emerging technologies and techniques can take part in it. The perspectives presented in this chapter provide at least three ways of reading the book:

1) a trail that follows the cognitive-to-technical process of understanding going from very conceptual levels to very technological ones (therefore reading Chapter 2, then Chapter 1, then Chapter 4 and then Chapter 3);

2) a trail that follows key requirements for a sound approach to CSE (therefore reading Chapter 1, then Chapter 2, then Chapter 4 and then Chapter 3);

3) a trail that follows the structural aspect of computational frameworks going from core components to periphery (therefore reading Chapter 3, then Chapter 4, then Chapter 1 and then Chapter 2).

It is very likely that students, domain researchers and professionals will find this volume increasingly interesting if they undergo several readings, adopting different trails from one reading to the other, thus grabbing more and more insights. Indeed, each of the book's chapters opens many research perspectives that call for further developments, leading to new research directions.

I.4. Bibliography

[ALV 10] ALVANCHI A., LEE S., ABOURIZK S., "Modelling framework and architecture of hybrid simulation and discrete event simulation for construction", *Computer Aided Civil and Infrastructure Engineering*, vol. 26 no. 2, pp. 1–15, 2010.

[ANG 06] ANGIOLINI F., CENG J., LEUPERS R. *et al.*, "An integrated open framework for heterogeneous MPSoC design space exploration", *Proceedings of the Conference on Design, Automation and Test in Europe*, pp. 1145–1150, 2006.

[ATK 03] ATKINSON C., KÜHNE T., "Model-driven development: a metamodeling foundation", *IEEE Software*, vol. 20, no. 5, pp. 36–41, 2003.

[BEN 98] BENJAMIN P., ERRAGUNTLA M., DELEN D. *et al.*, "Simulation modeling at multiple levels of abstraction", in MEDEIROS D., WATSON E., CARSON J. *et al.*, (eds), *Proceedings of the 1998 Winter Simulation Conference*, 1998.

[BER 00] BERTALMIO M., SAPIRO G., CHENG L.T. *et al.*, A framework for solving surface partial differential equations for computer graphics applications, CAM Report 00-43, UCLA, 2000.

[BRU 14] BRUNELIERE H., CABOT J., DUPE G. *et al.*, "Modisco: a model driven reverse engineering framework", *Information And Software Technology*, vol. 56 no. 8, pp. 1012–1032, 2014.

[CED 12] CEDENO W., ALEX S., JAEGER E., "An integrated data management framework for drug discovery – from data capturing to decision support", *Current Topics in Medicinal Chemistry*, vol. 12, no. 11, pp. 1237–1242, 2012.

[CHA 13] CHAHAL K., ELDABI T., YOUNG T., "A conceptual framework for hybrid system dynamics and discrete event simulation for healthcare", *Journal of Enterprise Information Management*, vol. 26 no. 1/2, pp. 50–74, 2013.

[CUI 12] CUI T., FRANCHETTI F., "A multi-core high performance computing framework for probabilistic solutions of distribution systems", *IEEE Power and Energy Society General Meeting*, 2012.

[DAV 93] DAVIS P.K., HILLESTAD R., "Families of models that cross levels of resolution: issues for design, calibration and management", *Proceedings of the 25th conference on Winter Simulation*, ACM, New York, pp.1003–1012, 1993.

[DOR 02] DORST L., MANN S., "Geometric algebra: a computational framework for geometrical applications", *IEEE Computer Graphics and Applications*, vol. 22, no. 4, pp. 58–67, 2002.

[FAY 96] FAYYAD U., PIATETSKY-SHAPIRO G., SMYTH P., "Knowledge discovery and data mining: towards a unifying framework", in SIMOUDIS E.E., HAN H., FAYYAD U., (eds), *Proceedings of the Second International Conference on Knowledge Discovery and Data Mining*, AAAI Press, Portland, 1996.

[FER 98] FERRARI A., "JPVM: network parallel computing in Java", *Concurrency: Practice and Experience*, vol. 10, nos. 11–13, pp. 985–992, 1998.

[FLA 10] FLAMM C., ULLRICH A., EKKER H. *et al.*, "Evolution of metabolic networks: a computational framework", *Journal of Systems Chemistry*, vol. 1, no. 1, pp. 1–4, 2010.

[FLE 13] FLETCHER C.W., HARDING R., KHAN O. *et al.*, "A framework to accelerate sequential programs on homogeneous multicores", *IFIP/IEEE 21st International Conference on Very Large Scale Integration (VLSISoC)*, 2013.

[FUG 93] FUGGETTA A., "A classification of CASE technology", *Computer*, vol. 26, no. 12, pp. 25–38, 1993.

[FUJ 98] FUJIMOTO R., "Time management in the high level architecture", *Simulation*, vol. 71, no. 6, pp. 388–400, 1998.

[GAC 03] GACHET A. "Software frameworks for developing decision support systems – a new component in the classification of DSS development tools", *Journal of Decision Systems*, vol. 12, no. 3, pp. 271–281, 2003.

[GAM 95] GAMMA E., HELM R., JOHNSON R. *et al.*, *Design Patterns – Elements of Reusable Object-Oriented Software*, Addison-Wesley, 1995.

[GAS 09] GASTON D., HANSEN G., NEWMAN C., "MOOSE: a parallel computational framework for coupled systems of nonlinear equations", *Nuclear Engineering and Design*, vol. 239, no. 10, pp. 1768–1778, 2009.

[HIL 04] HILL C., DELUCA C., BALAJI V., *et al.* "Architecture of the Earth System Modeling Framework (ESMF)", *Computing in Science and Engineering*, vol. 6, no. 1, pp. 18–28, 2004.

[LEE 03] LEE J-K., LEE M-W., CHI S-D., "DEVS/HLA-based modeling and simulation for intelligent transportation systems", *Simulation*, vol. 79, no. 8, pp. 423–439, 2003.

[LEE 99] LEE W., STOLFO S., MOK K., "A data mining framework for building intrusion detection models", *Proceedings of the IEEE Symposium on Security and Privacy*, pp. 120–132, 1999.

[MER 13] MERSHAD K., ARTAIL H., "A framework for secure and efficient data acquisition in vehicular ad hoc networks", *IEEE Transaction on Vehicle Technologies*, no. 62, pp. 536–551, 2013.

[MPI 94] MPI FORUM, "MPI: a message-passing interface standard", *The International Journal of Supercomputer Applications and High Performance Computing*, no. 8, pp. 169–173, 1994.

[ODE 14] ODEN J.T., "Predictive computational science", *IACM Expressions*, no. 35, pp. 2–4, June, 2014.

[OMG 01] OBJECT MANAGEMENT GROUP, The common object request broker: architecture & specification v2.5, Technical report, 2001.

[ONE 11] O'NEILL B., RIEDL M., "Toward a computational framework of suspense and dramatic arc", *Proceedings of the 4th International Conference on Affective Computing and intelligent interaction*, vol. part I, Springer-Verlag Berlin, Heidelberg, pp. 246–255, 2011.

[PAL 12] PALPANAS T., "A knowledge mining framework for business analysts". *SIGMIS Database*, vol. 43, no. 1, pp. 46–60, 2012.

[PAT 01] PATEL S.J., LUMETTA S.S., "Replay: a hardware framework for dynamic optimization", *IEEE Transactions on Computers*, vol. 50, no. 6, pp. 590–608, 2001.

[PUE 99] PUERTA A., EISENSTEIN J., "Towards a general computational framework for model-based interface development systems", *Knowledge-Based Systems*, vol. 12, no. 8, pp. 433–442, 1999.

[RAY 11] RAY J., ARMSTRONG R., SAFTA C. *et al.*, "Computational frameworks for advanced combustion simulations", in ECHEKKI T., MASTORAROS E. (eds), *Turbulent Combustion Modeling: Advances, Trends and Perspective*, Springer-Verlag, Netherlands, 2011.

[REI 14] REINEKE J., TRIPAKIS S., "Basic problems in multi-view modeling", *Tools and Algorithms for the Construction and Analysis of Systems*, vol. 8413, pp. 217–232, 2014.

[ROY 08] ROY B., GRAHAM T.C.N., "An iterative framework for software architecture recovery: an experience report", *European Conference on Software Architecture*, Springer, Berlin, Heidelberg, pp. 210–224, 2008.

[SMA 13] SMARSLY K., HARTMANN D., LAW K.H., "A computational framework for life-cycle management of wind turbines incorporating structural health monitoring", *Structural Health Monitoring – International Journal*, vol. 2, no. 4, pp. 359–376, 2013.

[SOC 98] SOCHEN N., KIMMEL R., MALLADI R., "A general framework for low level vision", *IEEE Transaction on Image Processing*, vol. 7, no. 3, pp. 310–318, 1998.

[STE 09] STEINBERG D., BUDINSKY F., PATERNOSTRO M. *et al.*, *Eclipse Modeling framework*, 2nd ed., Addison-Wesley, 2009.

[TAO 09] TAO W-K, CHERN J-D., ATLAS R. *et al.* "A multiscale modeling system: developments, applications, and critical issues", *Bulletin of the American Meteorological Society*, vol. 90, no. 4, pp. 515–534, 2009.

[VAN 05] VAN DONGEN B., MEDEIROS A., VERBEEK H. *et al.*, "The ProM framework: a new era in process mining tool support", in CIARDO G., DARONDEAU P. (eds), *Application and Theory of Petri Nets*, Springer, Berlin, 2005.

[VIL 13] VILLARROYA S., VIQUEIRA J.R.R., COTOS J.M. *et al.*, "GeoDADIS: a framework for the development of geographic data acquisition and dissemination servers", *Computers & Geosciences*, vol. 52, pp. 68–76, 2013.

[YAN 08] YANG C-T., CHEN S-Y., "A multi-site resource allocation strategy in computational grids", *Advances in Grid and Pervasive Computing*, vol. 5036, pp. 199–210, 2008.

[ZEI 00] ZEIGLER B.P., KIM T.G., PRAEHOFER H., *Theory of Modeling and Simulation: Integrating Discrete Event and Continuous Complex Dynamic Systems*, Academic Press, Boston, 2000.

[ZEI 76] ZEIGLER B.P., *Theory of Modelling and Simulation*, Wiley, New York, 1976.

[ZEI 84] ZEIGLER B. P., *Multifacetted Modelling and Discrete Event Simulation*, Academic Press, New York, 1984.

1

How Can Modeling and Simulation Help Engineering of System of Systems?

Sociotechnological systems can be characterized as Systems of Systems (SoSs). Typically, they are not anywhere near optimal performance for societal objectives. While individual component systems (CSs) are capable, their organization into an overall system is lacking. The System of Systems Engineering (SoSE) problem is to design and implement a coordination mechanism that can provide the organization needed to move the overall system toward more optimal performance. In this chapter, we discuss negative and positive emergence and provide a layered architecture framework for positive emergence. We show how the System Entity Structure and Discrete Event System Specification (DEVS) can support development of models of SoS. Such models enable the design and testing of coordination mechanisms with built-in capability to improve over time, in order to overcome inevitable social barriers. Examples are discussed, including health care systems that have been called chaotic, disorganized, expensive and in need of a "team sport" approach.

1.1. Introduction

In a well-known paper, Maier [MAI 98] postulated five principal characteristics that distinguish today's sociotechnical systems composed of existing complex systems. Those systems are called SoSs and their constituents are called CSs. SoSs are characterized by five properties: operational independence of the components, managerial independence of the components, evolutionary development, geographic distribution, and

Chapter written by Bernard P. ZEIGLER.

emergent behavior where the latter is explained as: "The system performs functions and carries out purposes that do not reside in any component system. These behaviors are emergent properties of the entire SoS and cannot be localized to any component system. The purposes of the SoS are fulfilled by these behaviors".

Modeling and Simulation (M&S) can help systems engineers to develop models of SoSs and CSs that support design and testing of mechanisms that coordinate the interactions of the operational and managerially independent components. Social barriers will make such coordination mechanisms or rules hard to enforce, so M&S can also be marshaled to enable coordination mechanisms to improve over time. M&S Integrated Development Environments can help build and test such models as well as design, test and implement coordination and learning mechanisms.

Some of the SoS M&S stakeholders use cases include the following:

– SoS M&S system requirements development; both SoS and SoS M&S verification.

– Support consistent, traceable decomposition of SoS M&S system requirements to a ready-to-contract specificity, acquisition trade studies, quick-turn analyses, comparative analyses, system sensitivity studies, scenario planning, requirements verification and SoS system effectiveness analyses.

Stakeholders have diverse views about the nature and details of the "right" M&S capability, e.g. differing about the degree of needs for physics-versus effects-based modeling. This chapter takes the position that the "right" capability must fulfill an extensible set of SoS M&S stakeholders' use cases. The diversity of stakeholders' use cases suggests that a suite of M&S tools may best service current and future SoS M&S use cases. M&S capability should offer automatic scenario selection/construction in which suites of models cover the conceivable component models and alternatives of a system. Such a paradigm can be supported by a Modeling and Simulation Framework (MSF) and generative ontology [ZEI 13a, ZEI 16d] enabling selection and composition of the best SoS model to meet the on-demand intended use and objectives of a stakeholder user. Central to this approach is the System Entity Structure (SES), an M&S-specific ontology capable of representing the extensible family of all possible SoS designs and the extensible families of all possible SoS model architectures that could represent them. The SES supports the automatic aggregation of SoS elements, environments, threats and representations from repository into executable form.

For such capability, it is crucial to distinguish models from simulators – a model represents the essence of a System of Interest (SoI) needed for a simulation-based study or test, while a simulator is the platform for executing the model to generate its behavior in such studies or tests. This premise will be discussed more fully in the background section. Furthermore, the DEVS formalism [ZEI 76, WYM 67, WYM 93] provides a sound and practical foundation for working with models and simulators toward a solution to the problem at hand. Briefly stated, a DEVS model is a system-theoretic concept specifying inputs, states and outputs, similar to a state machine [MIT 12]. Critically different, however, is that it includes a time-advance function that enables it to represent discrete event systems, as well as hybrids with continuous components [NUT 11] such as SoS, in a straightforward platform-neutral manner. We stress the following points in anticipation of the upcoming discussion of our technical approach:

– DEVS formalizes what a model is, what it must contain and what it does not contain (experimentation and simulation control parameters are not contained in the model).

– DEVS is universal and unique for discrete event system models: any system that accepts events as inputs over time and generates events as outputs over time is equivalent to a DEVS: its behavior and structure can be described by DEVS.

– DEVS-compliant simulators execute DEVS models correctly, repeatably and efficiently. Closure under coupling guarantees correctness in hierarchical composition of components.

– DEVS models can be simulated on multiple different execution platforms, including those on desktops (for development) and those on high-performance platforms, such as multicore processors.

– A DEVS-compliant simulator for a multicore architecture will run DEVS-compliant compositions in a predictable manner that can exploit the performance attributes of the underlying architecture.

These claims are discussed in depth in publications such as [ZEI 00, NUT 11, MIT 12]. Furthermore, we showed that DEVS offers the bulleted benefits without undue performance degradation [ZEI 15b]. The Parallel DEVS Simulation Protocol provides close to the best possible performance except possibly where activity is very low or coupling among components is very small. Therefore, future well-designed DEVS-based simulators and models will greatly ease the difficulty of constantly upgrading technology migration.

1.2. Background

The MSF and Parallel and Distributed Simulation (PADS) [FUJ 99] theory will form the foundation for the sequel.

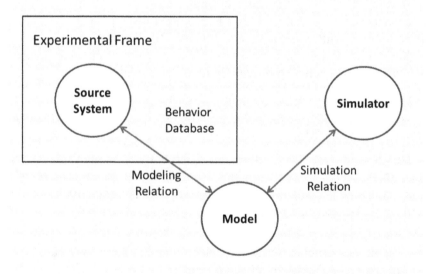

Figure 1.1. *Modeling and simulation framework*

1.2.1. *Modeling and Simulation Framework*

A MSF [ZEI 76, ZEI 00] presents entities and relationships of a model and its simulation (Figure 1.1). In the theoretical simulation usage, we employ here the MSF that differs from "distributed simulation frameworks" such as the Synchronous Parallel Environment for Emulation and Discrete-Event Simulation (SPEEDES) simulation engine [MET 03] for optimistic parallel processing on high-performance computers and networks. The MSF separates models from simulators as entities that can be conceptually manipulated independently and then combined in a relation, which defines correct simulation. The Experimental Frame (EF) defines a particular experimentation process, e.g. latin hypercube sampling for yielding model outcome measurements in accordance with specific analysis objectives.

Modular reuse, validity and executability of simulation compositions are common aspirations among enterprises regularly relying on M&S of SoI and SoSs throughout their lifecycles. Such enterprises, including those involved in SoS M&S and testing, invest significantly not only in development and experimentation, but also in verification and validation. The MSF helps clarify many of the issues involved in such activities. Mismatch between the simulation's time management policy and the model's time advance approach creates significant errors in even the simplest M&S. Simulation with relatively coarse discrete time advance for a discrete event model exemplifies these kinds of errors [NUT 08]. Distributed federations of discrete event and discrete time simulations with the High-Level Architecture (HLA) [NUT 04] are especially prone to conflicts between the intended, as-modeled event order and the implemented, as-simulated state-transition event order. Such conflict-based event causality errors in a tightly coupled SoS simulation may introduce significant behavior deviations from the correct result. The MSF underlies the DEVS Simulation Protocol that provides provably correct simulation execution of DEVS models, thereby obviating the above-mentioned conflicts as well as throwing light on the source of such conflicts in legacy simulations.

1.2.2. DEVS simulation protocol

The DEVS Simulation Protocol serves as the foundation of the proposed work in which the performance models to be developed will be simulated under this protocol. The protocol also provides the basis for an architecture in which legacy compositions, whether refactored or reengineered, can be mapped, thus we present some background here to clarify the upcoming proposed research.

The DEVS Simulation Protocol is a general distributed simulation protocol that prescribes specific mechanisms for:

– declaring who takes part in the simulation (component models = federates);

– declaring how federates exchange data;

– executing an iterative cycle that;

- controls how time advances (time management),

- determines when federates exchange messages (data exchange management),

- determines when federates do internal state updating (state update management).

The protocol guarantees correct simulation in the sense that if the federates are DEVS models, then the federation is also a well-defined DEVS coupled model. Distinct from HLA, the DEVS protocol prescribes specific time, data exchange and state update management processes.

To provide a more concrete description, we provide a reference implementation that represents in principle how all implementations work. A reference implementation of the DEVS Protocol, simulators and coordinators, specifies the following:

– each federate (component model) is assigned to a (distinct) simulator;

– the federation (coupled model) is assigned to a coordinator;

– the coordinator and simulators interact to realize the DEVS simulation protocol, i.e. the coordinator controls the execution of the basic iteration cycle by invoking the prescribed operations in the simulators' interface in the prescribed manner.

The reference implementation is not intended to be efficient – it provides a reference point to an unbounded set of possible equivalent implementations that can have desired performance properties.

There are numerous implementations of DEVS simulators (e.g. [MIT 12]). In particular, ADEVS [NUT 11] is the Parallel DEVS platform on which we plan to test the execution aspects of the proposed work. ADEVS is an open source implementation of the DEVS simulators that targets high-performance, multicore and multiprocessor computer systems. It uses a conservative parallel discrete event simulation algorithm to enable the parallel execution of DEVS models on these types of high-performance computing systems. These conservative algorithms are unique in the sense that they reproduce exactly the behavior of the DEVS reference simulators; this feature distinguishes ADEVS from the numerous other conservative simulation engines that are derived from the logical process approach to PADS (e.g. logical processes are the basis for the SPEEDES algorithm, which cannot reproduce in all circumstances the behavior of the DEVS reference simulators).

The ADEVS simulation is also distinguished by its support for both discrete event and continuous dynamic systems, both of which are simulated within the DEVS framework [NUT 12, NUT 14]. This capability is important to be able to simulate the interaction of subsystems characterized by discrete event dynamics (e.g. communication networks and command and control systems) and continuous, physical dynamics (e.g. the trajectories of ballistic missiles and their interceptors) within the above-mentioned simulation.

1.2.3. The system entity structure ontology framework

Our approach is based on the MSF framework, which is based on mathematical systems theory that offers a computational basis for application of M&S to systems engineering and that has become widely adopted for its support of discrete event, continuous and hybrid applications. A fundamental representation a of DEVS hierarchical modular model structures is the SES, which represents a design space via the elements of a system and their relationships in a hierarchical and axiomatic manner. SES is a declarative knowledge representation scheme that characterizes the structure of a family of models in terms of decompositions, component taxonomies and coupling specifications and constraints [ZEI 84]. As it has been described in a number of publications [PAW 16, ZEI 13b] the SES supports development, pruning and generation of a family of DEVS simulation models.

SES [ZEI 84] is a formal ontology framework, axiomatically defined, to represent the elements of a system (or world) and their relationships in hierarchical manner making a family of hierarchical DEVS models. Figure 1.2 provides a quick overview of the elements and relationships involved in a SES. Entities represent things that have existence in a certain domain. They can have variables that can be assigned a value within given ranges and types. An aspect expresses a method of decomposing an object into more detailed parts and is a labeled decomposition relation between the parent and children. MultiAspects are aspects for which the components are all of the one kind. A specialization represents a category or family of specific forms that a thing can assume. It is a labeled relation that expresses alternative choices that a system entity can take on.

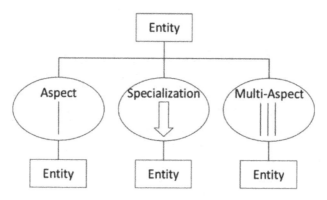

Figure 1.2. *Overview of SES items and relationships*

Figure 1.3 illustrates an SES developed for a Ballistic Missile Defense System (BMDS), for example an SoS. On the left is the SES of the BMDS showing specializations of SBIRS and TPY2 components. On the right is a viewer image of the simulation model generated by selecting high-resolution and high tracking capability for SBIRS and TPY2 components, respectively. This gives a quick look at how the SES represents a family of BDMS SoS simulation models and how particular model configurations are specified by selecting alternatives from choices (component system specializations). The EF represents the intended use of the models by (in this case) measuring the performance of the BDMS in an end-to-end manner. This EF computes SoS-embedded performance assessments of alternative system components as measured by their own performance level and the correlation of the component's participation with the overall system performance level. Stochastic Monte Carlo runs enable statistically significant estimation of performance measures and selection of the best compositions of CS.

1.2.4. *Pruning of the system entity structure*

The SES enables selection of:

– system of system configurations (SES "aspects");

– component system alternative functional and abstraction level choices (SES "specializations");

– numbers and configurations (recursively) of instances in multiple replications (SES "multiaspects").

Selection of such items entails cutting off alternative structures. Pruning is the term we apply to the process of making such selections (and concomitant removals). Selection rules can provide expert support for selections as well as the couplings and interfaces as appropriate for component configurations. Figure 1.4 illustrates pruning of the SES in Figure 1.3 for two of several available requirements. One type of study requirement is to determine the level of success in detecting and intercepting targets – this implies selecting an end-to-end representation of the BMDS with only sufficient resolution on each component to enable monitoring the message exchanges among components and scoring the efficiency of the handoff from along the sensor to intercept chain. In this case, the end-to-end system representation is retained but high-resolution versions of components are cut-off in favor of low-resolution equivalents.

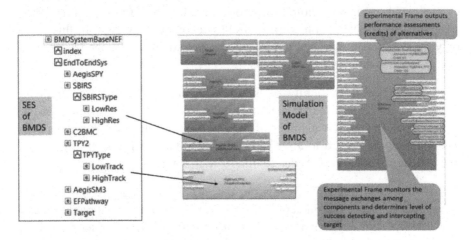

Figure 1.3. *An illustrative system entity structure of a BMDS*

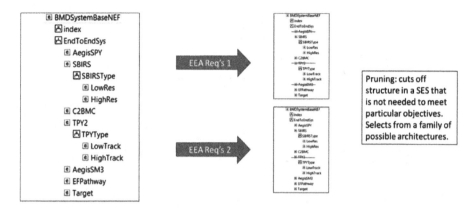

Figure 1.4. *Illustrating pruning of SES for the BMDS example. For a color version of this figure see, www.iste.co.uk/traore/frameworks.zip*

Multimissile battles underlie a type of study requirement that would require selecting the number of replications of opposing instances of end-to-end systems in battle encounters to estimate the probability of intercepting opposing missiles in such encounters. A high-resolution version of the command and control system (CBMC) would be selected to enable focus on its ability to manage the information and decision-making work load.

Another type of study requirement is to focus on target flight phases (e.g. simulate plume-to-hard body handover algorithms, navigation, guidance and control and endgame homing algorithms for boost-phase interceptor programs using abstractions of near-field phenomenology data. In this case, only the components needed in the phase under study are retained as well as one or more high-resolution versions.

A SES specifies a family of hierarchical, modular simulation models, each of which corresponds to a complete pruning of the SES. Pruning of the SES selects a particular member of the family of models to be synthesized. The mapping from SES to a DEVS-coupled model is depicted in Figure 1.5 and the transformation rules are summarized in Table 1.1.

In summary, the SES supports the automatic aggregation of SoS components and environments from repository into executable form. Importantly, this aggregation is aligned with analysis objectives and requirements to produce a pruned set of resources and scenarios, optimized for simulation execution on target computational platforms (multicore, cloud, etc.).

System Entity Structures   Pruned Entity Structures   Simulation Models (DEVS)

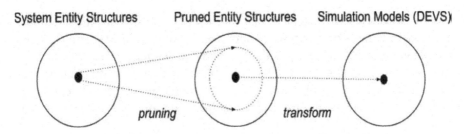

Figure 1.5. *Mapping of SES to DEVS models via pruning and transformation*

SES element	DEVS model
Entity	Atomic or coupled DEVS model
Aspect	Decomposition of a coupled model into DEVS models corresponding to the aspect's children. Specifies the coupling of input and output ports for information flow among the atomic/coupled models corresponding to the aspect's children
MultiAspect	Decomposition of a coupled model into corresponding DEVS models, each of which is derived from the aspect's single children entity
Specialization	A family alternative "plug-ins" for a DEVS model corresponding to the parent entity

Table 1.1. *Mapping SES elements to DEVS models*

1.3. Positive and negative emergence

In a fundamental characterization of emergence, Mittal and Rainey [MIT 15] contrasts *positive* emergence that fulfills the SoS purpose and keeps the constituent systems operational and healthy in their optimum performance ranges, from *negative* emergence that does not fulfill SoS purposes and manifests undesired behaviors such as load hot-swapping and cascaded failures. Their point is that with appropriate concepts, emergence can be harnessed, i.e. emergent behaviors can be controlled and designed by system engineers.

1.3.1. Negative emergence

Negative emergence was clarified in a little recognized report by Mogul [MOG 06], which presented a starting point of taxonomies of emergent *misbehaviors* and their *causes*. The context is software, particularly computer operating systems, but is generally suggestive.

Mogul focuses on system-level misbehavior that does not include bugs, component failures or "obviously" poor designs such as insufficient resource provision or not using best practice methods, techniques or algorithms. The causes are "built in" to the system, inherent in its design or implementation. As Rachel Madow would say, they are features not bugs. Of course, a component failure could trigger a manifestation of such a system-level design failure.

Some misbehaviors listed by Mogul are somewhat reformulated as:

– *Unanticipated resource contention*: Contention for resources that results in wasteful switching overhead such as thrashing in operating systems.

– *Unwanted synchronization or periodicity*: CS that were supposed to interact in ergodic unsynchronized fashion fall into synchronized periodic lock step.

– *Deadlock/livelock*: Components cannot move because of circular dependency (deadlock) or get in a loop while still active but where throughput decreases (livelock). Livelock differs from deadlock in that it is input dependent and can be relieved under reduced load.

– *Phase change*: The behavior of a system changes radically from desired normal modes to undesired failure modes when component behaviors exceed critical thresholds. For example, power drops cause networks to become sparsely connected.

Some causes Mogul enumerates are as follows:

– *Unexpected resource sharing*: Unplanned resource usage patterns arise.

– *Massive scale*: Large numbers of (possibly simple) components interact to give rise to complex global behavior.

– *Decentralized control*: Distributed systems that lack central controls can suffer from incomplete knowledge and delayed information.

– *Unexpected inputs or loads*: Small inputs can excite resonant frequencies and loads can exceed expected limits.

We can start associating misbehaviors with causes, singly or in combination, as presented in Table 1.2.

Misbehaviors/causes	Unexpected resource sharing	Massive scale	Decentralized control	Unexpected inputs or loads
Unanticipated resource contention	X		X	X
Unwanted synchronization or periodicity		X	X	X
Deadlock/livelock	X		X	X
Phase change		X	X	X

Table 1.2. *Some misbehaviors and causes in negative emergence*

Developing a comprehensive list of well-defined misbehavior characterizations and their possible causes can support mechanisms for detecting misbehaviors and curing systems of them (akin to debugging). Likewise, if we were able to characterize types of positive emergence or emergence in general, we would be able to implement Emergence Behavior Observers (EBO) [MIT 15, ZEI 16a, ZEI 16b] in infrastructures to offer services for querying component states and interactions in real time from executing simulations.

1.3.2. *Positive emergence*

If negative emergence is an unintended consequence of SoS design, then positive emergence should be a deliberate result of design that promotes it. For such an approach, we suggest the following trilayered architectural framework (Figure 1.6):

– *SoS Ecology*: The systems that will become CS of the SoS already exist as viable autonomous entities in an ecology; however, left unperturbed they would not emerge into the SoS under consideration.

– *Network supporting Pragmatic level of communication*: The ability to communicate among putative CS of the SoS, not only at technical level, but at a level that supports the coordination needed at the next level (this is the "Pragmatic" level vs. the underlying syntactic and semantic layers [ZEI 07]).

– *Coordination economics*: A compound term we introduce to refer to (1) the *coordination* required to enable the components to interact in a manner that allows emergence of the SoS with its own purposes, and (2) the economic conditions that enable emergence – the collective benefit that the

SoS affords versus the cost to individuals in their own sustainability to contribute to the SoS objectives.

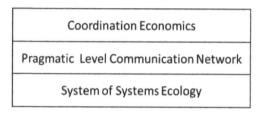

Figure 1.6. *Trilayered architecture for positive emergence*

As an analogy, consider an ant colony as a model of a SoS. Here, individual ants, members of the colony, are the putative components of the SoS. Prior to evolving collaborative foraging, ant species were part of a natural *ecology*, capable of surviving and reproducing – though not as robustly as in colonies. As the analogue of the second layer, *network supporting pragmatic level of communication*, we point to the communication enabled by the hormone they secrete while moving. Ants drop pheromone that can be detected by other ants. Trails form from pheromone deposits that accumulate and persist along high production paths and are subsequently followed to reduce search time to food sources. This mechanism of indirect coordination in which the environment is altered by an action that stimulates a next action is called stigmergy. Here, it illustrates the *coordination* needed to enable a SoS to emerge, i.e. a colony as a viable autonomous entity with its own survival imperatives. The *economic* cost of pheromone production capability must be overcome by increased survivability (fitness) afforded to individual ants by the colony.

1.4. Emergence in National Healthcare Systems

Health care in the United States can be considered to be in a state characterized by the lowest layer of the emergence conditions stack. It is a system of autonomous systems (consumers, providers, payers) able to survive, although at a very high cost to the national treasury. In Figure 1.6, we employ the trilayered architecture to suggest how health care might be reformed to emerge as a SoS that achieves much higher health care value, i.e. the same or better outcomes at significantly lower cost. For the *network supporting pragmatic level of communication*, we consider an information technology infrastructure that supports authorized access and exchange of all varieties of health-related information (e.g. patient treatment records and data on treatment results). Such an infrastructure does not exist today – although the Internet technology (web, cloud, etc.) provides technical interoperability among hospital and other information systems, common computerized processing of documents at the pragmatic level seems quite far off.

A modicum of such ability to exchange health information is at least necessary to support the *coordination* of health-related services needed to improve effectiveness, efficiency and focus resources where they are most needed. Value-based pricing and purchasing will enable government and insurers to pay for quality of outcomes achieved rather than the services that may or may not have contributed to such outcomes. Determination of value as quality of treatment per dollar of cost, and transparency to consumers and payers will enable competition and market forces to weed out poor performers and allow better performers to emerge into a high-quality/low-cost SoS.

1.4.1. *M&S-based design of health care service systems*

Based on the architecture just presented, we now discuss how M&S can be applied to design and implement the coordination layer at the level of reform involving radical restructuring of the ways in which multiple systems interact to deliver health care [WIC 08, BRA 07, AUG 14]. Indeed, health care delivery can be regarded as a *service system* that comprises service providers and clients working together to coproduce value in complex value chains. Following [SPO 11], we raise the question: Under what conditions, does a Healthcare Service System (HSS) improve itself, and how can we design such a system to improve in this manner?

Roughly our argument is as follows: A HSS is made up of humans and technology where for the foreseeable future, self-improvement will be primarily based on human understanding rather than machine learning. Artificial intelligence and cognitive computing, such as IBM's WatsonPaths [IBM 14], will be increasingly better at generating and evaluating hypotheses about improved treatments and other interventions. However, humans must make decisions about protocols, processes and procedures to actually put in place to improve health care delivery. Therefore, in order for a HSS to continually self-improve it must provide the right data and models to support human selection of alternatives likely to improve the quality of its services. It follows that:

a) there must be working definitions of *quality of service*, for example Porter's Healthcare Value, defined as outcome divided by cost [POR 13a];

b) there must be *systems implemented to measure*, in an ongoing manner, the elements of clinical and extraclinical interventions that can be aggregated to compute quality of service as defined;

c) likewise, there must be implemented systems that allow *alternative component configurations* (protocols, processes, procedures) to be continually tested [RIP 14];

d) there must be systems to *correlate measured quality* with component configurations to provide evaluations that humans can employ to help select the most promising options.

A prerequisite for such conditions to prevail in an HSS is that sufficient organization and infrastructure exists to support their implementation. Currently, most national health care systems do not meet this prerequisite. At the high end is health care delivery in the United States. Although the most costly in the world, it focuses on medical services and fails to include social services that are equally important in achieving good health outcomes [BRA 11]. U.S. health care has been diagnosed as consisting of loosely coupled, fragmented systems that are not sufficiently integrated or coordinated to provide high quality of service [AHR 09] or to enable self-learning [NSF 11]. At the low end, some national health care infrastructures are both underdeveloped and uncoordinated so that leap-frogging into 21st Century learning systems is critical to meeting the challenges of burgeoning populations (Traore, personal communication). In the middle, nationalized systems are better organized from the top down but still lack the infrastructure to experiment, measure and evaluate on the large scales required to implement self-improving HSSs.

Our focus in this chapter is to show how M&S can help design service infrastructures that introduce coordination and bring into play the conditions (a) through (d) for a self-improving HSS [ZEI 16c]. To do this, we discuss the application of the DEVS formalism [ZEI 00] to the design of self-improving HSSs. In particular, we discuss a concept of coordination models for transactions that involve multiple activities of CSs and coordination mechanisms implementable in the DEVS formalism. We show how SoSE concepts [JAM 08, BOA 06] enable formal representation that combines Porter's value-based care concepts [POR 13a] with pathway community HUB care coordination [RED 14d] to enable implementation of criteria for measurement of outcome and cost. This leads to a pathways-based approach to coordination of HSSs and to a proposed mechanism for continuous improvement of HSSs as learning collaborative SoSs.

The framework will be expressed at the fine grained level in which individual patents are explicitly represented because this is a level of analysis at which the metrics of quality and cost are fundamentally measured. However, means for aggregation of data to more abstract levels of analysis are also included to support generalization and quality improvement. In the sequel, we will point out the technical benefit that DEVS offers over other approaches. Finally, we will suggest how the paper offers a fertile framework for HSS of system engineering that can stimulate further research in both the underlying theory and its application.

1.4.2. Overview of DEVS methodology for coordination modeling

We begin with an introduction to DEVS M&S methodology that links DEVS thinking into the need for coordination in U.S. health care. With the intent of presenting a broad overview, the discussion is rather terse and relies on references to the literature and media to suggest where the reader can fill in the details [ZEI 14a]. Further exposition will be forthcoming as the paper proceeds. As illustrated in Figure 1.7, an SoS, which is a system composed of multiple complex systems, can be abstracted to a simulation model [ZEI 13a].

This is a DEVS model obtained by coupling together component models representing the systems components. The representative SoS model can be used to test mechanisms developed to coordinate transactions that cut across multiple CSs. Such component models can be derived by abstracting the features (activities, services, etc.) of the CS that are relevant to defining coordination mechanisms for cross-system transactions of interest [ZEI 14a]. SES is a hierarchical system representation framework that supports automated generation of the SoS simulation model by coupling together all component system models that have been selected from component models in a model base [KIM 13]. Then, after virtual testing in the SoS simulation, the same models can be implemented in net-centric information technology using the model-continuity properties of the DEVS framework. Such model-continuity allows simulation models to be executed in real time as software or hardware by replacing the underlying simulator engine [MIT 12]. Several M&S environments based on DEVS support design, testing and implementation of coordination mechanisms in an SoSE approach [ZEI 13b, SEO 14, ZEI 14a].

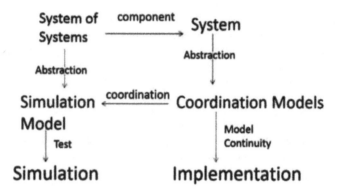

Figure 1.7. *Modeling and simulation methodology for coordination systems engineering*

1.4.3. Health care as a learning collaborative SoS

On the U.S. national level, a Learning Health System is being envisioned that lays out several requirements including one for a stable, certifiable, adaptable and self-improving system. A workshop on the topic raised such questions as: What is the relationship between health care delivery innovations, such as team practice and patient engagement, and the extent and quality of learning in such a system? NSF and Porter and Teisberg [NSF 11, POR 06] advocate radical reform of health care that requires that physicians reorganize themselves into Integrated Practice Units (IPUs) moving away from care that is currently based on specialties with associated hospital departments.

An IPU is centered on a medical condition defined as an interrelated set of patient medical circumstances best addressed in an integrated way. Porter's formulation for an IPU emphasizes knowledge acquisition and continuous improvement based on measurement of outcomes but does not provide a mechanism to do this. We will discuss a generalization of Porter's IPU concept based on DEVS and SoS concepts that lays the groundwork for application of DEVS to continuous improvement of HSSs.

First, we summarize and review some of the basic concepts required to formulate the continuous improvement problem for collaborative HSSs [MUZ 14a]. Table 1.3 defines features characteristic of continuous improvement and exemplifies them for multidisciplinary physician teams, characteristic of IPUs.

Characteristic feature	Definition	Multidisciplinary physician team manifestation
Enclosing system	SoS for which goal requires collaboration may enclose components of more than one identified system	Integrated Practice Unit
Component system	A component that participates in the enclosing system	Physician
Collaboration requirement	Description of the goal that requires collaboration	Each physician must provide his/her service to the assure successful treatments
Modularity	Component system has well-defined interfaces and its own contained state	Physicians within the same discipline can be interchanged to play the same role in a team
Specialization	Component Systems have variants that are interchangeable in the slot represented by the component. Typically, the variants represent the behavior characterized by the component in specialized manners	Physicians specialize via disciplines to play specific roles in a team
Variety at component level	The variants available for substitution alternatives in the component slot	Physicians schedules and participation in multiple teams provide variety in components
Outcome quality of service	Composite effect at the SoS level of an assignment of alternatives to component slots. This is the global behavior of the enclosing system, that is health care outcome to be evaluated	Some physicians work well with others, some do not. So selecting the best team composition for a given full cycle of patient care is a challenge
What constitutes a single trial	The time interval during which activity of components, global outcome and their correlation are evaluated as a single instance	Time spent by physician in full cycle of care rendered to a patient
Evaluation of trial	The evaluation of activity of components, global outcome and their correlation for a trial instance	Health care value (outcome per unit cost as will be defined in text)

Table 1.3. *Exemplifying features characteristic of continuous improvement in multidisciplinary physician teams*

While the table shows the elements needed for implementing continuous improvement strategies, it does not show how to employ these elements in a manner to implement such a strategy. We now turn to a proposal for such a strategy and its implementation.

1.5. DEVS coordination pathways

Craig and Whittington [CRA 11] present a care coordination framework aimed at improving care at lower cost for people with multiple health and social needs. Although such a framework provides a starting point, it does not afford a rigorous predictive model that takes account of emerging health information networks and electronic health records (EHRs). The Pathways Community HUB model is a delivery system for care coordination services provided in a community setting [AHR 11]. The model is designed to identify the most at-risk individuals in a community, connect them to evidence-based interventions and measure the results [RED 14]. Community care coordination works at the SoS level to coordinate care of individuals in the community to help address health disparities including the social barriers to health.

The Pathways Community HUB model is a construct that enforces threaded distributed tracking of individual clients experiencing certain pathways of intervention, thereby supporting coordination of care and fee-for-performance based on end-to-end outcomes [ZEI 14d, ZEI 14c]. As an essential by-product, the pathway concept also opens up possibilities for system level metrics that enable more coherent transparency of behavior than previously possible, therefore greater process control and improvement re-engineering.

Zeigler [ZEI 14a] developed a *Coordination Model* that abstracts essential features of the Pathways Community HUB model [RED 14] so that the kind of coordination it offers can be understood and employed, in a general SoS context. This allows development of an M&S framework to design, test and implement such coordination models in a variety of SoS settings, exemplified by health care, that presents the issues that such coordination models address. Formalization provides a firm basis for capitalizing on the transparency that is afforded by the Pathways Community HUB model [ZEI 14b]. Such pathways were represented as DEVS atomic models with implementation in the form of an active calendar that combines event-based control [ZEI 89], time management and data architecture capabilities [ZEI 16d]. Furthermore, such DEVS pathways can become components of coupled models, thereby enabling activation of successors and sharing of information. Such pathway models represent steps in a pathway as states that can constrain steps to follow each other in proper succession with limited branching as required; external input can represent the effect of a transition from one step to the next due to data entry. Moreover, temporal aspects of the pathways including allowable duration of steps can be directly represented by the DEVS atomic model's assignment of residence times in states.

1.5.1. Individual-based coordination of cross-system transactions

In the following, we review the theory developed by Zeigler [ZEI 14a, ZEI 16c] as a basis for the main discussion to come. In the kind of coordination considered here, there are multiple service providers (CS) whose activities must be brought together in different ways to serve different clients. In the as-is situation, a client is to a large extent responsible for selecting, sequencing and scheduling encounters with providers. Since multiple activities are located in different CS, the client needs to traverse several activities across different systems to complete a *cross-system transaction*. Thus, an adequate coordination model is characterized by the following requirements:

– coordination design must define cross-system transactions and criteria for their successful completion;

– one or more cross-system transactions may be assigned to a client;

– a coordination agent must aim to assure that clients will successfully complete their assigned transactions;

– coordination tracks the completion state and provides accountability for success/failure of the client and coordination agent in completing assigned transactions;

– coordination allows computing the costs of sets of cross-system transactions by accumulating the costs of activities involved in such sets.

1.5.2. *Pathways as coordination models*

Viewed as coordination models as just defined, coordination pathways provide concrete means to:

– define steps in terms of goals and subgoals along paths to complete cross-system transactions;

– test for achievement and confirmation of pathway goals and subgoals;

– track and measure progress of clients along the pathways they are following;

– maintain accountability of the compliance/adherence of the individual and responsible coordination agent.

An information technology implementation of such Pathways can provide abilities to:

– query for the state of a client on a pathway;

– query for population statistics based on aggregation of pathway states for individuals;

– support time-driven activity-based costing [KAP 04] based on pathway steps and their completion times.

1.5.3. *Atomic pathways models*

Three aspects of atomic pathway models to note are as follows:

– their primary role is to request and receive data about a main goal and benchmarks (or subgoals) accomplishment – we will call these Questions and Answers;

– bounded times are given for answers to be received;

– accomplishment of the main goal is decidable after a finite time in the sense that the model is guaranteed to wind up (and remains) in one of three classes of states: known success, known failure or incomplete. In the last state, the model explicitly reports that it is unknown whether the goal has been achieved or not.

In the following, we illustrate how atomic pathway models are formally defined as a class of DEVS models. *An atomic pathways model is a* DEVS [ZEI 00]:

$$M = <X, S, Y, \delta_{int}, \delta_{ext}, \lambda, ta>$$

where,

- X is the set of input values;
- S is a set of states;
- Y is the set of output values;
- $\delta_{int}: S \rightarrow S$ is the *internal transition* function;
- $\delta_{ext}: Q \times X \rightarrow S$ is the external transition function, where

  - $Q = \{(s,e) | s \in S, 0 \leq e \leq ta(s)\}$ is the total state,
  - e is the time elapsed since last transition,

  - $\lambda: S \rightarrow Y$ is the output function,
  - $ta: S \rightarrow R_0^+$ is the *time advance* function.

Table 1.4 gives the definition of the sets and functions in the specification.

An example of an atomic model representing a pathway with one goal is given in Figure 1.8. The model starts in state WA (for waitForActivate), which is passive (its time advance, ta is infinity). When an activate is received (input ports are noted by ?, output ports by !), the model transitions to the initialization state I, which is a transient state (ta = 0). This state immediately outputs the question, GoalReached and transitions to the state WG (waitForGoal.) In this state, the model can receive answers Yes or No and eventually enter passive states S (Success) and F (Failed), respectively (S is entered after an Activate output is generated from state SY). However, WG has a finite time advance, TN, so that it transitions to states Inc (incomplete) if it does not receive one of the Yes or No answers within this interval. Since Inc is a passive state, it is easy to see that, as required, this simple model always winds up (and remains) in one of the three states S, F or Inc.

Set and functions	Explanation
$X = Answers \cup \{Activate\}$ $Y = Queries \cup \{Activate\}$	Inputs are answers received by sending out queries plus the ability to send and receive an activation signal.
$S = \{s_0, s_1, s_2, s_3, \ldots s_N\} \cup \{Success,$ $Failure, Incomplete, End\}$	The states form a sequence starting with subscript 0 and ending with subscript N where N is an even integer. In addition, there are states for successful and unsuccessful completion, as well as an incomplete state (see text).
$ta(s_0) = \infty$	The starting state is a passive state (waits for input).
$\delta_{ext}(s_0, e, Activate) = s_1$	Upon receiving an activation signal, the initial state goes to the first indexed state.
$\delta_{int}(s_i) = s_{i+1}$ $ta(s_i) = 0$ $\lambda(s_i) \in Queries$	The first indexed state and all odd indexed states immediately output queries and transition to the next even indexed state.
$\delta_{ext}(s_{i+1}, e, ans) = s_{i+2})$ for $ans \in$ $Answers$ $ta(s_{i+1}) = T_{i+1}$ $\delta_{int}(s_{i+1}) = Incomplete$	An even indexed state waits for a specified time interval (parameter of the model); if it receives an expected answer within that time, it transitions to the next odd indexed state; otherwise (a timeout situation), it transits to the incomplete state.
$\delta_{ext}(s_N, e, ans) \in \{Success, Failure\}$ $ta(s_N) = T_N$ $\delta_{int}(s_N) = Incomplete$	In the last state of the sequence and answer indicates either success or failure. Timeout is again to the incomplete state.
$ta(Success) = 0$ $\lambda(Success) = Activate$ $\delta_{int}(Success) = End$ $ta(End) = \infty$ $ta(Failure) = \infty$ $ta(Incomplete) = \infty$	Success outputs an activation signal and transitions to the passive end state. Failure and incomplete states are passive. None of these states accepts input.

Table 1.4. *Definition of the sets and functions in atomic pathway model*

Following the methodology in Figure 1.7, such a specification can be automatically transformed into a component of a simulation model and tested through simulation as well as implemented in actual software to function in an actual HSS setting.

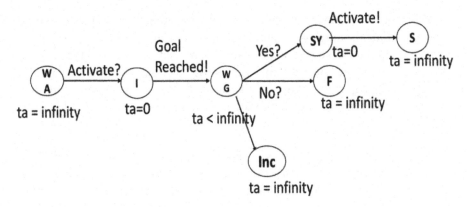

Figure 1.8. *Atomic pathway models*

1.5.4. *Coupled pathways models*

Coupling atomic pathway models to compose coupled models enables us to coordinate the behavior of multiple concurrent pathways. For simplicity in exposition, coupling will be limited to activations by one pathway of one or more others. The DEVS formalism's closure under coupling will assure that the resultant is a DEVS model. More than that, we can show that the resultant is also expressible as an atomic pathway model, establishing closure under coupling when restricted to the subset of DEVS defined as pathway models. The following property is essential to such closure:

Finite termination property:

– For any atomic pathway model, there is a finite time T, such that the model reaches, and passivates, in any one the three types of states: Success, Failed or Incomplete within time T after initialization.

– For any coupled pathway model, there is a finite time T, such that all the components of the model reach, and passivate, in any one of the three types of states: Success, Failed or Incomplete within time T after initialization.

Zeigler [ZEI 14a] proved the Finite Termination Property and the closure under coupling of pathway models. Examples of coupled pathway models are presented in the upcoming discussion.

Many of the features discussed above are common to both coordinated care and clinical pathways commonly employed in hospital settings [OZC 11, DEB 07]. However, coordinated care pathways are focused on accomplishment of steps, with associated accountability and payment schemes. Consequently, they specify tests for accomplishment and time bounds within which such tests must be satisfied (see [ZEI 14c] for more details).

As indicated, we must have working definitions of *quality of service* and there must be *systems implemented to measure*, in an ongoing manner, the elements of clinical and extraclinical interventions that can be aggregated to compute quality as defined. We turn to formalizing quality as the quotient of health value delivered divided by the cost to deliver it.

1.5.5. Porter's IPU

As indicated, Porter and Teisberg [POR 06] advocate radical reform of health care that requires that physicians reorganize themselves into IPUs moving away from care that is currently based on specialties with associated hospital departments (geriatrics, obstetrics, etc.). As formulated by Porter [POR 10] and Porter and Lee [POR 13b], an IPU is centered on a medical condition defined as an interrelated set of medical circumstances best addressed in an integrated way. Examples of IPUs are those centered on asthma, diabetes, congestive heart failure and so on. These target a cluster of related adverse health conditions that includes the most common co-occurring complications. As such, the IPU may bring together a host of specialists and services needed to treat the target in an integral manner – as a team rather than as a collection of individual entities. This assemblage of individual independent entities into a single collaborative organization fits the pattern of SoS and motivates research to provide a firm basis for such integration. The IPU delivers all the services needed for the target condition that are organized into an *end-to-end interaction* with the patient called a full cycle of care covering a Care Delivery Value Chain (CDVC). Here, "Value" is defined as health outcome achieved per dollar of cost. The critical requirement is that such a metric be quantifiable so that it can be compared by the patient – or surrogate payer such as insurance company – to the equivalent number offered by the competition. Much like the increase in value in a manufacturing process, the Value Chain is a linked set of activities that increase value (i.e. contribute to the outcome) from the initiation of the care cycle to its termination.

Porter and Teisberg [POR 06] formulate the CDVC as a chain of activities that constitutes the architectural blueprint of the integrated team-based practice unit. From an SoS perspective, the CDVC specifies the organization of its components and their coupling. Adopting this perspective allows us to generalize the application of the CDVC concept to HSSs beyond the IPU. To do this, we interpret Porter's discussion of requirements for a properly constituted CDVC as:

– the set and sequence of activities are aligned with value – generally, value should increase and cannot decrease, later activities cannot have lesser value than precursors. Taken together, the activities must achieve the desired outcomes;

– the activities have the right scopes to cover the target medical cluster of conditions and to minimally overlap;

– the activities form a coherent whole with seamless handoffs from one to the other – this will ultimately minimize process delays and "dropping the baton" [RUD 14].

Porter provides examples of CDVCs for particular targeted medical conditions following the template below. The main value-producing activities are shown along the bottom row. Supporting activities are shown in the first column. In principle, any of the supporting activities can be paired with the main activities. Furthermore, supporting activities can also operate across the full care cycle, e.g. knowledge development can concern the interrelationship of the main activities.

	Preventing	Diagnosing	Preparing	Intervening	Recovering/ rehabilitating	Managing
Knowledge development						
Informing						
Measuring						
Accessing						
Monitoring						

Table 1.5. *Template for instantiating a care delivery value chain*

The template will be illustrated in relation to the design of a coordinated care HSS for HIV-AIDS.

As indicated, the CDVC enables computing the numerator in the value definition by defining how outcomes are produced. As shown in the template, the CDVC also includes measurement and other activities that cut across the outcome producing activities and that are capable of observing the behavior of the outcome producing activities. The key guiding principle is that "whatever is measured tends to improve" [POR 13b]. The denominator in the value quotient is the cost attributable to the activities that produced an outcome. This requires that the activities are sufficiently granular to support activity-based cost analysis. We now consider how both numerator and denominator are formalized in our DEVS-based approach.

Porter's Outcome Measurement Hierarchy [POR 10, POR 13a] provides a comprehensive basis for the measurement system. The hierarchy has three tiers relating to health status, process of recovery and sustainability of health. Each tier has two parts. Tier 1 concerns survival and degree of health or recovery, Tier 2 concerns time to recovery and disutility of care or treatment process and Tier 3 concerns sustainability of health or recovery including nature of recurrences and long-term consequences of therapy. Porter [POR 10] emphasizes that measuring the full set of outcomes that matter is indispensable to better meeting patients' needs and a powerful vehicle for lowering health care costs. As illustrated in Figure 1.9, the form of the SES shows the HealthCareSystem composed of three components: Health Status Achieved, Process of Recovery and Sustainability of Health. Following Porter's approach, each of these is divided into the two types of measures illustrated in the figure. The basic event-based pathways models implement specific measures into the six slots to flesh out the full measuring system. Before discussing the SES in more detail, we note that we employ the DEVS pathway representation for the Measurement System along the lines of Porter's Outcome Hierarchy design approach. We can define a comprehensive set of outcome dimensions, and specific measures based on the event-based experimental frame methods implementable using DEVS. *Following the Pathways Coordination model, it allows tracking patients through the full cycle of care to accumulate actual costs of care (not how they are charged, which currently is often done in arbitrary fashion).*

1.5.6. *Pathways-based cost measurement*

Qualitatively, an activity is a label assigned to a state trajectory over an interval. Events that start and end such activity cause discrete changes in the state of the system when formulated in discrete event terms. A quantitative measure of activity was provided by the framework presented by Hu and Zeigler [HU 13]. In this approach, the *activity* of a DEVS model is simply measured by the count of its state transitions. Thus, as a DEVS model, activity of a pathway over a time interval is measured by the number of state transitions that occurred in the interval. The activity of the overall system is estimated by the aggregation of all individual pathway activities. When activity is aggregated over all individuals that traversed a component, we get an estimate of the component's activity. These measures can be subindexed by pathway to rank the overall system activity from most active to least active pathway, thereby providing insight into how the system is being utilized. Further subindexing by factors such as condition treated, patient attributes and source of client referral enables analysis of the variation due to such factors (see [ZEI 14c] for details).

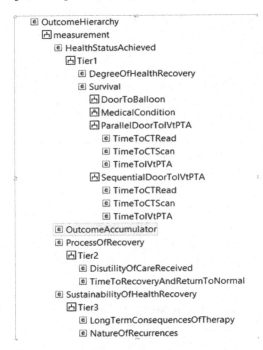

Figure 1.9. *SES for outcome hierarchy*

Pathway activity can be correlated to personnel and resource expenditures to calculate costs using time-driven activity-based costing [KAP 04]. Distributions of activity can be used to inform continuous improvement as will be discussed soon.

As indicated, systems must be implemented that allow *alternative component configurations* (protocols, processes, procedures) to be continually tested. The SES Outcome Hierarchy in Figure 1.9 offers an example of alternative architectures for "door-to-critical-interventions". These are shown as specializations for survival in Figure 1.9 that can be selected as appropriate for different medical conditions. For example, a heart attack implementation [BRA 06] might use only a single atomic pathway model to measure door-to-balloon times and survival rates. In contrast, a stroke implementation might employ one of the sequential or parallel alternative architectures for its time-lost-is-brain-lost interventions. The SES supports automated generation of the SoS model once all selections have been made from component models in a model base.

1.6. Example: coordinated HIV-AIDS care system model

The continuity spectrum of HIV-AIDS intervention spans HIV diagnosis, full engagement in care, receipt of antiretroviral therapy and achievement of complete viral suppression (Figure 1.10). However, Gardner *et al.* [GAR 11] estimates that only 19% of HIV-infected individuals in the United States have been treated to the point where their virus is undetectable. This occurs because achievement of an undetectable viral load is dependent on overcoming the barriers posed by patients "falling through the cracks" in traversing each of the sequential stages shown in Figure 1.10. The authors conclude that recognition of the "pipeline" and support for successful handoff of patients from stage to stage is necessary to achieve a substantial increase in the successfully treated HIV population. Figure 1.10 depicts the stages of care continuity roughly assigned to both clinical and extraclinical domains, and their alternation between the two domains (shown cycling from 1 to 4).

Here, we consider the approach of formulating the DEVS pathways discussed above for stages 1 and 3 to form an IPU. In addition, DEVS pathways are proposed for stages 2 and 4, which are similar to those of the pathways community HUB. Using a DEVS coupled model, the clinical domain pathways are interfaced to the extraclinical ones. The objective is that patients are handed-off from one DEVS Pathway to the next without being dropped from care. Such cross-organization care pathways require sufficient EHR system and health information technology networking support to track and monitor patients as they traverse the treatment pipeline [VAN 13, RUD 14]. Recall that this will require definition of goals and subgoals along paths to complete cross-system transactions, testing for achievement and confirmation of pathway goals and subgoals, tracking and measuring progress of patients along the pathways they are following, and maintaining accountability of compliance and adherence. The implementation of such IT can then provide a "dashboard" for viewing the overall disposition of patients through the complete cycle of continuity of care required for successful HIV-AIDS treatment.

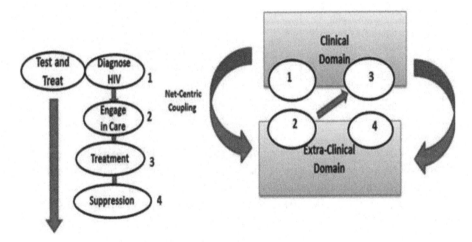

Figure 1.10. *HIV-AIDS continuity of care pathway model*

Although formulated for IPUs, the criteria for a well-specified CDVC apply generally to healthcare SoSs. Table 1.6 applies the criteria to provide a basis for achieving a CDVC for the HIV-AIDS example in Figure 1.10. The main value chain activities appear in this example as Diagnosis, Engagement, Treatment and Suppression. They are organized in a sequence and must satisfy the criteria given for well-defined CDVCs in order to support value-based health care.

Criteria for well-specified CVDC	Application to HIV-AIDS
The set and sequence of activities are aligned with value	– Set: Diagnosis, engagement, treatment, suppression – Sequence: Shown in Figure 1.10 – Earlier stages must be completed before later stages – All four stages must be completed for positive outcome
The activities have the right scopes to cover the target medical cluster of conditions and to minimally overlap	– Diagnosis determines presence of HIV – HIV presence triggers engagement – Engagement enables treatment – Treatment enables suppression
The activities form a coherent whole with seamless handoffs from one to the other – minimize process delays and "dropping the baton"	– The sequence in Figure 1.10 is minimal connection at pathway level – Must be implemented faithfully with minimal delays at service level – *Must assure transfer without dropping patient*

Table 1.6. *Illustrating criteria for well-specified CDVC for HIV-AIDS*

The generalization of value chain concepts from IPUs to HSS in general allows us to achieve a synthesis that applies to HSS with both clinical and extraclinical aspects. The synthesis combines Porter's value-based concepts of CDVC and Outcome Hierarchy with pathways concepts that support implementation capabilities such as individual end-to-end goal-based tracking[1].

---

1 Other criteria for implementing a CDVC that need to be accounted for in a family of models at one or more levels of abstraction include the following: (i) the right information is collected, utilized and integrated across the care cycle. This requires that sufficient Electronic Health Records and Health Information networking are available to support to track and monitor patients as they traverse the continuity of care pipeline. (ii) The HHS includes members with the appropriate skills for the activities in the CDVC. Providers in clinical (doctors, nurses, lab technicians) and in extraclinical domains (CHWs, supervisors, etc.) are assumed skilled for their current role; otherwise, there is the need to be trained in order to collaborate in coordinated HSS. (c) Activities in the CDVC are performed in the right locations and facilities, e.g. clinical activities are retained in current locations, community-based locations are found for extraclinical activities.

1.6.1. *Pathways-based learning system implementation*

Returning to the conditions that allow a HSS to continually self-improve, we have laid the foundation with a working definition of quality of service, DEVS pathway models for systems implemented to measure and compute quality of service in an ongoing manner, as well as systems that allow alternative component configurations (protocols, processes, procedures) to be continually tested. Finally, we noted that there must be systems to *correlate measured quality* with component configurations to provide evaluations that humans can employ to help select the most promising options. In this regard, continuous improvement in health care can be productively viewed as a specific kind of adaptation over time of a collaborative system whose components can take on alternative variants [FEI 14]. The goal is to keep improving the value (outcome/cost) of the system's CDVC by finding combinations of component variants that produce high-value outcomes. In the following, we present an approach based on the application of credit assignment and activity-based selection of component alternatives to successively increase the level of collaboration needed to produce progressively higher valued outcomes. In this regard, Muzy *et al.* [MUZ 13] identifies three layers of an activity-based adaptive system:

– Time-Driven Activity-Based Costing using a built-in system for measurement of component activity and performance (outcome value);

– Activity Evaluation and Storage: Using the built-in detection mechanisms of level 1, activity can be measured as the fractional time that a component contributes to the outcome. Correlating contribution with outcome, a credit can be attributed to components. Such a measure of performance of components can be memorized in relation to the experimental frame, or context, in which it transpired;

– Activity awareness: Feedback of the activity-outcome correlation to inform the selection of combinations of component variants so as to drive the system toward increased performance.

This kind of adaptive system differs from other simulation-based optimization systems (see, e.g. [SWI 00]). It also differs from supervised learning (e.g. [SUT 98]) in that here learning is based on correlation between the activity of CS and the behavior achieved at the SoS composition level.

Muzy and Zeigler [MUZ 14a] describe a system that implements these layers in a simulation that involves finding winning combinations of players on a hockey team. This demonstration shows how to automatically rate CS and compose them according to the experimental frames in which they are placed. To achieve this objective, simulation-based evaluation is performed (goals scored) of hierarchical components (a team is composed of attack and defense combinations, such "lines" are composed of players, and players are composed from basic skills.). Activity-based performances consist of the correlation between component activity and behavior evaluated at the team level[2]. Performances of hierarchical components are stored in a hierarchical model base. A simulation-based stochastic search is achieved based on the performance model base. Correlation between the activity of a component and corresponding composition outcome is referred to the credit assignment problem. The credit of components is used to bias their selection. Activity-based credit assignment (ACA) was shown to (1) apply to any level in the hierarchy of components within any experimental frame, (2) converge on good compositions much faster than a repository-based random search and (3) automatically synthesize an SoS from a model base, thus enabling reusability of highly rated components in compositions.

Pathway coordination models lend themselves to support critical features of such learning systems. As mentioned before, DEVS pathways enable time-driven activity-based costing [KAP 04] based on pathway steps and their completion times. Recall that, as a DEVS model, the activity of a pathway over a time interval is measured by the number of state transitions that occurred in the interval. We can estimate a component's activity by aggregating the pathway activities over all individuals that traversed the component during an interval. Moreover, since pathways include outcome measurement, they enable correlation of activity and performance (CDVC value) for each individual. Aggregation over individual traversals of components yields estimates of activity–outcome correlation for components. Components or variants that do not perform well in this measure are candidates for replacement by other alternatives that can replace them. Such activity-based performance correlation and feedback exhibits the continuous improvement characteristic of an evidence-based learning health care system advocated by Porter and others.

---

2 Sports offer a domain in which a plethora of performance statistics at both the player and team levels are being applied to select players and compose winning teams (see, e.g. [SHE 13]).

1.6.2. ACA applied to HIV-AIDS example

Table 1.7, exemplifying features characteristic of continuous improvement in collaborative health care, sets up the basis for application of the ACA-based continuous improvement to the case of the HIV-AIDS continuity of care.

Characteristic feature	HIV-AIDS continuity of care manifestation
Component system	Stage of continuity of care (diagnosis, engagement, treatment, suppression)
Collaboration requirement	Stages form pipeline, each stage must follow the prior one and set up the next one
Modularity	Stages are distinct from each other having different goals and (conceptually) well-defined interfaces
Specialization	Alternative processes for stages are specialized to support the different goals of the respective stages
Variety at component level	A continuous improvement approach would seek to alter subprocesses and/or internal couplings (information flows) to provide requisite variety
Outcome quality of service	Not all combinations of pipeline component variations will work together
What constitutes a single trial	Time consumed by a stage in patient traversal of the pipeline
Evaluation of trial	The number of stages successfully traversed by a patient

Table 1.7. *Exemplifying features characteristic of continuous improvement in continuity of care*

As indicated, the stages of Continuity of Care (Diagnosis, Engagement, Treatment and Suppression) form a pipeline in that each stage must follow the prior one and set up the next one. As shown in Figure 1.11, the stages can be viewed as CSs coupled together in the overall SoS, which represents the pipeline. The stages are distinct from each other, having different goals and alternative processes for each stage specialized in order to support the goals of the stage. Not all combinations of pipeline component variations will work to achieve the overall SoS goal of enabling patients to traverse the full pipeline, i.e. to receive the complete intervention required by continuity of care. Each patient constitutes the basis for a trial with the evaluation of a trial being how many stages the patient successfully traversed. The overall objective of continuous improvement is to increase the number of successful patient pipeline traversals, ideally to reach 100%, but with an objective of reaching a level of 65% [GAR 11]. Muzy and Zeigler [MUZ 14b] consider a family of pipeline-coupled models with alternatives selected from an independent identically distributed random process. They proved that for such a pipeline, the activity-based credit assignment converges to an equilibrium distribution in which the best alternative at each stage has a credit that exceeds the others at that stage. This result offers an analytic confirmation to support the simulation results of [MUZ 14a] and a basis to propose that the implementation of a continuous improvement strategy based on ACA, such as that discussed above, will prove successful in real applications.

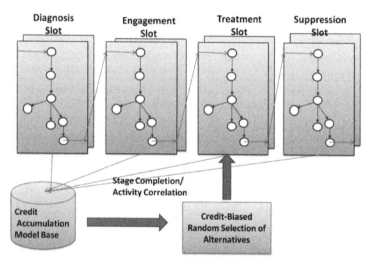

Figure 1.11. *Illustrating implementation. Activity-based credit assignment in the HIV-AIDS SoS*

1.6.3. *Current state of DEVS framework for a coordinated learning health care system*

At least three types of users for M&S environments can be distinguished: M&S developers, general M&S users and M&S expert professionals [ZEI 13a]. For M&S developers, DEVS-based methodology offers a comprehensive approach to SoSE that other simulation languages and tools do not provide. Mittal and Risco-Martín [MIT 12] and Denil [DEN 13] provide extensive discussion of DEVS unified process and end-to-end methodology involving design, verification and deployment in net-centric environments. General M&S users are interested in using the models and associated products of environments in ways not necessarily envisioned when they were produced. Specialized simulation packages for particular world views (see, e.g. for hospital simulation, [GUN 12]) are able to quickly synthesize usable models with matching user interfaces. However, the capabilities of such tools fall short as their styles and domains of application are exceeded. On the other hand, in new domains such as HSS and other service systems, generic DEVS environments, such as MS4 Me [ZEI 13a], enable development of novel concepts and mechanisms with accompanying user interfaces that meet the new challenges but also take more time to mature. M&S Expert Professionals are interested in the internals of models and in research and development of new technologies. As an open formalism, DEVS fosters environments that support transparent model presentation and comprehension as well as scrutiny of the environment's features and the theory that supports them.

The DEVS comprehensive methodology, illustrated in Figure 1.7, underlies the development of pathways-based self-improving HSS architecture models. It proceeds along parallel paths of HSS simulation model development, coordination and learning submodels, testing of the submodels in the simulation model and implementation of the submodels within actual health care environments. Progress in the development can proceed independently along segments where the paths do not intersect. As of this writing, the development of the simulation is in progress where initial steps have taken the form of formalization of the basic pathways concept and analysis of real data using this formalization. As reported in [ZEI 14c] and [ZEI 14b], the formalization in terms of DEVS provides enabled temporal analysis that would be difficult to undertake with conventional biostatistics.

The development of HSS simulation models is proceeding with a focus on West Africa (personal communication). Ebola is a non-standard infectious disease due to its very high contamination potential – simple contact is enough, unlike HIV-AIDS that requires fluid transmission inside the body. It is likely that the Ebola spreading in Sub-Saharan Africa is amplified by the combination of cultural behavior (social interactions during burials, rural life and closeness, incautious approach to the management of unhealthy people, etc.), population dynamics (temporary and permanent movements between villages and cities, rapid growth of population, etc.) and environmental conditions favorable to virus propagation (ambient temperature, source in diet, etc.). Classical models of infection spread are therefore not adequate. Models must be developed that are fine grained to account for cultural behavior, population dynamics and local climate and environmental conditions. Such models are not easily analyzed using conventional simulation languages and require DEVS-based methodologies. Hierarchies of scale for both systems (e.g. local units, regional centers and organization; cell, individual, population) and processes (e.g. contamination, disease, epidemic) were designed using the SES. Couplings among system components within and between levels implement cross-aspect interactions along the lines defined by Seck and Honig [SEC 12]. The development of this model family is in process and will be employed to test pathway coordination approaches to Ebola outbreak control in West Africa.

Finally, the model continuity path shown in Figure 1.7 was used to partially automate the mapping of pathway models into Web-based implementation. Figure 1.12 shows the browser interface that supports selection of SES documents such as the one for HIV-AIDS as shown, pruning by making selections from the alternatives for each slot and executing the model to obtain activity-based credit evaluations of alternatives [SEO 15]. At this point, a simplistic test simulation lies behind the evaluation but eventually an actual trial within an HSS, or indeed any service system could be implemented.

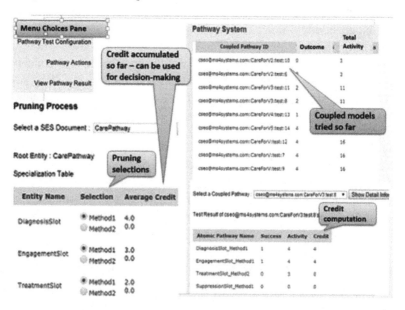

Figure 1.12. *Web-based implementation of pathways*

1.7. Conclusions and further research

An AHRQ/NSF workshop [AH 09] envisioned an ideal health care system that is unlike today's fragmented, loosely coupled and uncoordinated assemblage of CS. The workshop concluded that "an ideal (optimal) health care delivery system will require methods to model large scale distributed complex systems". Improving the health care sector presents a challenge in that the optimization cannot be achieved by suboptimizing the CS, but must be directed at the entire system itself. On the other hand, health care has been compared to manufacturing with the premise that many of the same techniques can be transferred to it. However, complex patient flows, numerous human resources and dynamic evolution of patient's health state motivated Augusto and Xie to develop Petri-net-based software for modeling, simulation and activity planning and scheduling of health care services [AUG 14]. Their goal was to provide a mathematical framework to design models of a wide range of medical units of a hospital in order to model and simulate a wide range of health care services and organizations and to support such a design with a Unified Modeling Language/business process modeling interface for decision makers. In contrast, our concern here is not within the hospital but at the SoSs level where hospitals interact with other components such as physicians, community workers, social services and health plan payers.

At the SoS level, care coordination is the organization of all activities, both clinical and extra-clinical, among the individual patient and providers involved in the patient's care to facilitate the appropriate delivery of health care services. In this chapter, we discussed a trilayer architecture for promoting positive emergence intended to be applicable to sociotechnical systems of systems generally whatever the specific domain. Although simple in form, it is intended to provide the right core abstraction that can be refined and extended as needed in the domain application intended. The characteristic taxonomy of misbehaviors and causes provides an initial framework for planning to minimize the effects of negative emergence in the SoS under consideration. For example, future work can examine the characteristic taxonomy in the context of the emerging health care system to suggest EBO that can detect problems in advance, reducing their potential surprise.

We then expanded upon an SoSE formalization and simulation modeling methodology for a more in-depth application of DEVS coordination pathways to re-engineer HSSs. In particular, we discussed a concept of coordination models for transactions that involve multiple activities of CS and coordination pathways implementable in the DEVS formalism. We showed how SoS concepts and pathway coordination models enable a formal representation of complex health care systems requiring collaboration, including Porter's integrated practice concepts, to enable implementation of his criteria for measurement of outcome and cost. This lead to a pathways-based approach to coordination of such systems and to the proposed mechanism for continuous improvement of health care systems as learning collaborative SoSs.

The US President's Council on Science and Technology [PCA 14] advocates that the U.S. health care industry adopt a systems engineering approach used in other industries to improve the health data infrastructure and boost overall quality and delivery of care. Among the recommendations (three of five): are those relating to technology development:

– align payment incentives and reported data with better outcomes for individuals and populations;

– speed up efforts to create a health data infrastructure in the United States;

– provide national leadership in systems engineering through increased data supply to better gauge performance, understand the health of a community and analyze broader regional or national patterns.

Our results support the contention that understanding health care as an HSS and applying SoSE methods based on simulation modeling helps to address these recommendations. The pathways and activity-based evaluation of components provides a basis for aligning payment incentives for subgoal completion. Distributed individual-based tracking enabled by pathways provide a basis for effective design of a health data infrastructure. Increased data supply on the community level enabled by extraclinical Pathway Hubs and the analysis supported by M&S will enable better understanding of health care delivery as a self-improving service system.

1.8. Bibliography

[AHR 09] AHRQ/NSF, "Industrial and systems engineering and healthcare: critical areas of research", Report, Workshop co-sponsored by the Agency for Healthcare Research and Quality, 2009.

[AHR 11] AHRQ, "Connecting those at risk to care: the quick start guide to developing community care coordination pathways", available at https://innovations.ahrg.gov/sites/default/files/guides/CommHub_QuickStart.pdf, 2011.

[AUG 14] AUGUSTO V., XIE X., "A modeling and simulation framework for health care systems", *IEEE Transactions on Systems, man, and cybernetics: Systems*, vol. 44, no. 1, pp. 30–46, 2014.

[BOA 06] BOARDMAN J., SAUSER B., "System of systems – the meaning of of", *IEEE/SMC International Conference on System of Systems Engineering*, IEEE, Los Angeles, 2006.

[BRA 06] BRADLEY E.H., HERRIN J., WANG Y. *et al.*, "Strategies for reducing the door-to-balloon time in acute myocardial infarction", *New England Journal of Medicine*, vol. 355, pp. 2308–2320, 2006.

[BRA 07] BRAILSFORD S.C., "Tutorial: advances and challenges in healthcare simulation modeling", *Proceedings of the 2007 Winter Simulation Conference 2007 (WSC'07)*, pp. 1436–1448, 2007.

[BRA 11] BRADLEY E.H., ELKINS B.R., HERRIN J. *et al.*, "Health and social services expenditures: associations with health outcomes", *BMJ Quality and Safety*, vol. 20, no.10, pp. 826–831, 2011.

[CRA 11] CRAIG C., WHITTINGTON D., "Care coordination model: better care at lower cost for people with multiple health and social needs", *IHI Innovation Series White Paper*, Institute for Healthcare Improvement, Cambridge, available at: www.IHI.org, 2011.

[DEB 07] DE BLESER L., DEPREITERE R., DE WAELE K. *et al.*, "Defining pathways", *Journal of Nursing Management*, vol. 14, pp. 553–563, 2007.

[DEN 13] DENIL J., Design, verification and deployment of software intensive systems: a multi-paradigm modelling approach, PhD Thesis, University of Antwerp, 2013.

[FEI 14] FEI T., LAILI Y., LIU Y. *et al.*, "Concept, principle and application of dynamic configuration for intelligent algorithms", *IEEE Systems Journal*, vol. 8, no. 1, pp. 28–42, 2014.

[FUJ 99] FUJIMOTO R.M., *Parallel and Distribution Simulation Systems,* John Wiley & Sons, Inc., New York, 1999.

[GAR 11] GARDNER E.M., MCLEES M.P., STEINER J.F. *et al.*, "The spectrum of engagement in HIV care and its relevance to test-and-treat strategies for prevention of HIV infection", *Oxford Journals Medicine Clinical Infectious Diseases*, vol. 52, no. 6, pp. 793–800, 2011.

[GUN 12] GUNAL M.M., "A guide for building hospital simulation models", *Health Systems*, vol. 1, pp. 17–25, 2012.

[HU 13] HU X., ZEIGLER B.P., "Linking information and energy-activity-based energy-aware information processing", *Simulation*, vol. 89, no. 4, pp. 435–450, 2013.

[IBM 14] IBM, "Watsonpaths", available at http://www.research.ibm.com/cognitive-computing/watson/index.shtml, 2014.

[JAM 08] JAMSHIDI M., *Systems of Systems – Innovations for the 21st Century*, John Wiley and Sons, Hoboken, 2008.

[KAP 04] KAPLAN R.S., ANDERSON S.R., "Time-driven activity-based costing", *Harvard Business Review*, vol. 82, no. 11, pp. 131–138, 2004.

[KIM 13] KIM K.S., CHOI C.B., KIM T.G., "Multifaceted modeling and simulation framework for system of systems using HLA/RTI", *Proceedings of the 16th Communications & Networking Symposium (CNS '13)*, SCS International, San Diego, Article 4, 2013.

[MAI 98] MAIER M.W., "Architecting principles for systems-of-systems", *Systems Engineering*, vol. 1, no. 4, pp. 267–284, 1998.

[MET 03] METRON INC., SPEEDES User's Guide, Solana Beach, 2003.

[MIT 12] MITTAL S., RISCO-MARTÍN J.L., "DEVS net-centric system of systems engineering with DEVS unified process", *CRC-Taylor & Francis Series on System of Systems Engineering*, Boca Raton, 2012.

[MIT 15] MITTAL S., MOON I.C., SYRIANI E. (eds.)., "Harnessing emergence: the control and design and emergent behavior in system of systems engineering", *Summer Computer Simulation Conference*, Chicago, pp. 1–10, 2015.

[MOG 06] MOGUL J.C., "Emergent (mis)behavior vs. complex software systems", HP Labs Tech Reports, available at http://www.hpl.hp.com/techreports/ 2006/ HPL-2006-2.pdf, 2006.

[MUZ 13] MUZY A., VARENNE F., ZEIGLER B.P. *et al.*, "Refounding of activity concept? Towards a federative paradigm for modeling and simulation", *Simulation*, vol. 89, no. 2, 2013.

[MUZ 14a] MUZY A., ZEIGLER B.P., "Activity-based credit assignment heuristic for simulation-based stochastic search in a hierarchical model-base of systems", *IEEE Systems Journal*, vol. 99, pp. 1–14, 2014.

[MUZ 14b] MUZY A., ZEIGLER B.P., "Conjectures from simulation learning on series and parallel connections of components", *Proceedings of EMSS*, 2014.

[NSF 11] NSF, "Toward a science of learning systems: the research challenges underlying a national scale learning health system, findings from a multidisciplinary workshop supported by the National Science Foundation", Report, available at http://healthinformatics.umich.edu/sites/default/files/files/uploads/NSF%20Report %20Ver%2011.11.13.pdf, 2011.

[NUT 04] NUTARO J., SARJOUGHIAN H.S., "Design of distributed simulation environments: a unified system-theoretic and logical processes approach", *Simulation*, vol. 80, no. 11, pp. 577–589, 2004.

[NUT 08] NUTARO J., "On constructing optimistic simulation algorithms for the discrete event system specification", *ACM Transactions on Modeling and Computer Simulation*, vol. 19, no. 1, pp. 1–21, 2008.

[NUT 11] NUTARO J., *Building Software for Simulation: Theory and Algorithms with applications in C++*, John Wiley & Sons, Hoboken, 2011.

[NUT 12] NUTARO J., KURUGANTI P.T., PROTOPOPESCU V. *et al.*, "The split system approach to managing time in simulations of hybrid systems having continuous and discrete event components", *Simulation*, vol. 88, no. 3, pp. 281–298, 2012.

[NUT 14] NUTARO J., "An extension of the OpenModelica compiler for using Modelica models in a discrete event simulation", *Simulation*, vol. 90, no. 12, pp. 1328–1345, 2014.

[OZC 11] OZCAN Y.A., TÀNFANI E., TESTI A., "A simulation-based modeling framework to deal with clinical pathways", *Proceedings of the 2011 Winter Simulation Conference*, in JAIN S., CREASEY R.R., HIMMELSPACH J. *et al.* (eds), *IEEE*, pp. 1190–1201, 2011.

[PAW 16] PAWLETTA T., SCMIDT A., ZEIGLER B.P. *et al.*, "Extended variability modeling using system entity structure ontology within MATLAB/simulink", *Proceedings of SCS International SpringSim/ANSS*, SCS, Pasadena, pp. 62–69, 2016.

[PCA 14] PCAST, "Better health care and lower costs: accelerating improvement through systems engineering", President's Council of Advisors on Science and Technology Report To The President, available at http://www.white.house.gov/sites/default/files/microsites/ostp/PCAST/pcast_systems_engineering_in_health care_-_may_2014.pdf, 2014.

[POR 06] PORTER M.E., TEISBERG E.O., *Redefining Health Care: Creating Value-based Competition on Results*, Harvard Business Review Press, Boston, 2006.

[POR 10] PORTER M.E., "What is value in health care?", *New England Journal of Medicine*, vol. 363 no. 26, pp. 2477–2481, 2010.

[POR 13a] PORTER M.E., Value-based health care delivery: integrated practice units, and outcome and cost measurement, available at https://www.google.com/url?sa=t&rct=j&q=&esrc=s&source=web&cd=1&cad=rja&uact=8&ved=0CB8QFjAA&url=http%3A%2F%2Fwww.hse.ie%2Feng%2Fservices%2Fnews%2Fnewsfeatures%2Fmasterclass%2Fprogramme%2FValueBasedHealthCareDelivery.pdf&ei=rgK-U-fiBoOPyAS_r4CYCA&usg=AFQjCNGt6UFwowQRZnLy7PNqRvxb4g5zGg&sig2=_vi4WIPJCFo6NCFlT8aoAA, 2013.

[POR 13b] PORTER M.E., LEE T.H., "The strategy that will fix health care", *Harvard Business Review*, vol. 91, no. 10, pp. 50–70, 2013.

[RED 14] REDDING S., CONREY E., PORTER K. *et al.*, "Pathways community care coordination in low birth weight prevention", *Maternal and Child Health Journal*, vol. 18, no. 6, pp. 1–8, 2014.

[RIP 14] RIPPEL FOUNDATION, "Can simulation modeling fill knowledge gaps about health care?", available at http://www.rethinkhealth.org/the-rethinkers-blog/can-simulation-modeling-fill-knowledge-gaps-about-health-care/, 2014.

[RUD 14] RUDIN R., DAVID S., BATES W., "Let the left hand know what the right is doing: a vision for care coordination and electronic health records", *Journal of the American Medical Informatics Association*, vol. 21, no. 1, pp. 13–16, 2014.

[SEC 12] SECK M.D., HONIG H.J. "Multi-perspective modelling of complex phenomena", *Computational & Mathematical Organization Theory*, vol. 18, no. 1, pp. 128–144, 2012.

[SEO 14] SEO C., KANG W., ZEIGLER B.P. *et al.*, "Expanding DEVS and SES applicability: using M&S kernels within IT systems", *Symposium on Theory of Modeling & Simulation – DEVS (TMS/DEVS) SpringSim*, San Diego, 2014.

[SEO 15] SEO C., ZEIGLER B.P., KIM D., "Integrating web-based simulation on IT systems with finite probabilistic DEVS", *Symposium on Theory of Modeling & Simulation SpringSim*, San Diego, 2015.

[SHE 13] SHEA S.M., BAKER C.E., *Basketball Analytics: Objective and Efficient Strategies for Understanding How Teams Win*, CreateSpace Independent Publishing Platform, Lake St Louis, 2013.

[SPO 11] SPOHRER J., MAGLIO P.P., BAILEY J. *et al.*, "Steps toward a science of service systems", *Computer*, vol. 40, no. 1, pp. 71–77, 2011.

[SUT 98] SUTTON R., BARTO A., *Reinforcement Learning: An Introduction (Adaptive Computation and Machine Learning)*, MIT Press, Boston,1998.

[SWI 00] SWISHER J.R., HYDEN P.D., JACOBSON S.H. *et al.*, "A survey of simulation optimization techniques and procedures", *Proceedings Winter Simulation Conference*, vol. 1, pp. 119–128, 2000.

[VAN 13] VAN HOUDT S., HEYRMAN J., VANHAECHT K. *et al.*, "Care pathways across the primary-hospital care continuum: using the multi-level framework in explaining care coordination", BMC Health Services, available at http://www. biomedcentral.com/1472-6963/13/296, 2013.

[WIC 08] WICKRAGEMANSIGHE N. *et al.*, "Health care system of systems"; in: JAMSHIDI M. (ed), *Systems of Systems – Innovations for the 21st Century*, John Wiley & Sons, Hoboken, 2008.

[WYM 67] WYMORE A.W., *A Mathematical Theory of Systems Engineering: The Elements*, John Wiley & Sons, New York, 1967.

[WYM 93] WYMORE A.W., *Model Based Systems Engineering*, CRC Press, Boca Raton, 1993.

[ZEI 76] ZEIGLER B.P., *Theory of Modelling and Simulation*, John Wiley & Sons, New York, 1976.

[ZEI 84] ZEIGLER B.P., *Multifacetted Modelling and Discrete Event Simulation*, Academic Press, New York, 1984.

[ZEI 89] ZEIGLER B.P. "The DEVS formalism: event based control for intelligent systems", *Proceedings of the IEEE*, vol. 77, no. 1, pp. 27–80, 1989.

[ZEI 00] ZEIGLER B.P., KIM T.G., PRAEHOFER H., *Theory of Modeling and Simulation: Integrating Discrete Event and Continuous Complex Dynamic Systems*, 2nd ed., Academic Press, Boston, pp. 510, 2000.

[ZEI 07] ZEIGLER B.P., HAMMONDS P., *Modeling & Simulation-Based Data Engineering: Introducing Pragmatics into Ontologies for Net-Centric Information Exchange*, Academic Press, Boston, 2007.

[ZEI 13a] ZEIGLER B.P., SARJOUGHIAN H.S., *Guide to Modeling and Simulation of Systems of Systems*, Springer, London, 2013.

[ZEI 13b] ZEIGLER B.P., SEO C., KIM D., "System entity structures for suites of simulation models", *International Journal of Modeling, Simulation, and Scientific Computing*, vol. 4, no. 3, p. 1340006, 2013.

[ZEI 14a] ZEIGLER B.P., "The role of modeling and simulation in coordination of health care", *Proceedings of SIMULTECH*, Vienna, available at http://vimeo. com/105849693, 2014.

[ZEI 14b] ZEIGLER B.P., REDDING S.A., "Formalization of the pathways model facilitates standards and certification", available at http://www.innovations.ahrq. gov/content.aspx?id=4097, 2014.

[ZEI 14c] ZEIGLER B.P., CARTER E.L., REDDING S.A. *et al.*, Care coordination: formalization of pathways for standardization and certification, available at http://www.rockvilleinstitute.org/files/Care_Coordination_Formalization_of_Pathwa ys_for_Standardization_and_Certification.pdf, 2014.

[ZEI 14d] ZEIGLER B.P., CARTER E.L., REDDING S.A. *et al.*, "Pathways community HUB: a model for coordination of community health care", *Population Health Management*, vol. 17, no. 4, pp. 199–201, 2014.

[ZEI 15a] ZEIGLER B.P., NUTARO J., "Towards a framework for more robust validation and verification of simulation models for systems of systems," *Journal of Defense Modeling and Simulation: Applications, Methodology, Technology*, vol. 1, 3 no. 1, pp. 3–16, 2015.

[ZEI 15b] ZEIGLER B.P., NUTARO J.J., SEO C., "What's the best possible speedup achievable in distributed simulation: Amdahl's law reconstructed", *DEVS TMS, SpringSim*, Alexandria, 2015.

[ZEI 16a] ZEIGLER B.P., "Some M&S perspectives on emergence in systems of systems. M&S of complexity in intelligent, adaptive and autonomous systems", *MSCIAAS SpringSim*, 2016.

[ZEI 16b] ZEIGLER B.P., "A note on promoting positive emergence and managing negative emergence in systems of systems", *The Journal of Defense Modeling and Simulation: Applications, Methodology, Technology*, vol. 13, no. 1, pp. 133–136, 2016.

[ZEI 16c] ZEIGLER B.P., "Discrete event system specification framework for self-improving healthcare service systems", *IEEE Systems of Journal*, vol. 99, pp. 1–12, 2016.

[ZEI 16d] ZEIGLER B.P., REDDING S.A., LEATH B.A. *et al.*, "Guiding principles for data architecture to support the pathways community HUB model", *EGEMS*, Washington DC, vol. 4, no. 1, p. 22, 2016.

2

Multidisciplinary, Interdisciplinary and Transdisciplinary Federations in Support of New Medical Simulation Concepts: Harmonics for the Music of Life

The role of modeling and simulation (M&S) to capture and provide knowledge in an executable form is becoming common practice. Various disciplines are encoding their knowledge already in computational support tools such as databases and ontologies. Using M&S to gain insight into the dynamic aspects of the respective systems is a logical next step. Many challenges of today's research, however, require more than one discipline contributing to a solution. Medical simulation is one example. This chapter discusses the various levels of disciplinary collaboration, the implications for simulation-based solutions and introduces hybrid simulation and reference modeling as current state-of-the-art solutions.

2.1. Introduction

Denis Noble's book "The Music of Life – Biology beyond the Genome" [NOB 08] helped introduce the idea for Systems Biology worldwide to biologists, including the medical simulation community. The traditional reductionist's view is reducing the organism into progressively finer and finer components to understand the interactions on the lowest levels and reconstruct the system back from these new insights. Noble shows that this

Chapter written by Andreas TOLK.

approach falls short when looking at complex organism, such as the human body, composed of several levels: organs, tissue, cellular, subcellular, pathways, proteins and genes. There are feed-downs and upward feeds between all these levels, so that a systemic approach is needed to understand the organism.

The cognitive challenge is that several disciplines have to be brought together to support these activities. In multidisciplinary approaches, the disciplines remain more or less as they are, they just share information with each other that is integrated into the knowledge base of each discipline. In interdisciplinary research, a certain challenge is approached by two or more disciplines as a common problem that needs to be solved. Data and functionality are shared and create domains in which the participating disciplines are highly interwoven. Finally, transdisciplinary approaches are creating new common knowledge that is transcending and transforming, creating a new approach that systemically integrates the knowledge components, and even creating new knowledge.

Recent research on interoperability and composability of simulation systems is based on the mathematical rigor of Model Theory. Using the Levels of Conceptual Interoperability Model (LCIM) and its mathematical interpretation, this contribution shows how data can be aligned and processes synchronized to create a set of tools that enable multi-, inter- and transdisciplinary federations in support of multilevel, multiscope and multiresolution simulations supporting the system biology approach envisioned by Denis Noble.

This chapter is based on the invited presentation on these topics during the 2015 African University of Science and Technology (AUST) conference. We will discuss what the different levels of disciplinary collaboration are, and what the implications for simulation systems can be derived from these insights. In order to do so, the processes of M&S – *What are Models? What are Simulations?* – will be defined. This will help to answer the question of why simulation-based collaboration between disciplines is often so hard. To clearly differentiate between complete reference models and consistent conceptual models and use these as the basis for hybrid simulation is a possible solution to create a solution that allows the support of systems biology: Orchestrating the "Music of Life".

This chapter is focusing on presenting ideas and research trends. As such, it is mainly intended to contribute to discussions and help to create a research agenda to address issues and align solutions. It is neither exclusive nor complete, not even a presentation of research ideas. It is a collection of ideas and challenges for the new generation of simulation engineers and the invitation to contribute to the development of more inclusive simulation approaches.

2.2. Multi-, inter- and transdisciplinary approaches

Science and engineering are conducted within several disciplines, although the proper criteria for organizing knowledge into disciplines is still open to debate. However, different disciplines can be distinguished by their topics of interests, the way they understand knowledge (ontology), the way they gain knowledge (epistemology), the methods and tools they are using and other often very practical criteria. In order to cope with complexity, science applied the principle of analyzing and describing a complex phenomenon by breaking them apart into smaller and simpler subsystems on a more fundamental level for many years. This principle of reductionism supported the idea of several independent disciplines well, but in recent years, the need to address problems systemically and holistically brought experts from several disciplines together to collaborate on solving problems.

The degree of collaboration of these experts and the disciplines can differ significantly. Stock and Burton [STO 01] introduced definitions for multidisciplinarity, interdisciplinarity and transdisciplinarity: In multidisciplinary approaches, experts from various disciplines are working together on a common question or topic of interest. Each discipline remains unchanged but simply contributes its knowledge, methods and expertise. When common tools are developed and the participating disciplines start to link to each other instead of juxtaposing, the effort becomes interdisciplinary. Permanent bridges between the disciplines are established. Finally, when the participating disciplines are systematically integrated to create new knowledge components in transcending and transgressing form, a new transdisciplinary effort emerges.

Figure 2.1. shows a comparison of these categories of disciplinarity. In multidisciplinary projects, the collaboration is deconflicted by clearly defined domains of responsibility and synchronized by the exchange of terms of a common controlled vocabulary. In interdisciplinary projects, common domains of mutual interest are identified in which the work is orchestrated by sharing methods and tools. In transdisciplinary projects, the borders between the disciplines vanish and a new discipline is born, in which all elements of the old disciplines are collaborating in a well-orchestrated manner, each part being applied to the biggest advantage of the new body of knowledge.

Like many other scientific disciplines, biology has been defined by reductionism: instead of evaluating and analyzing highly complex phenomena and systems, biologists focused on simpler and more fundamental subcomponents in order to find sufficient explanations about how these subsystems work. Recently, however, the need for more inclusive system approaches required to look for multi-, inter- and transdisciplinary approaches in biology in general, including computational biology. This motivates us to look at M&S support in more detail, and in particular at the question for implications of the various disciplinary approaches for M&S.

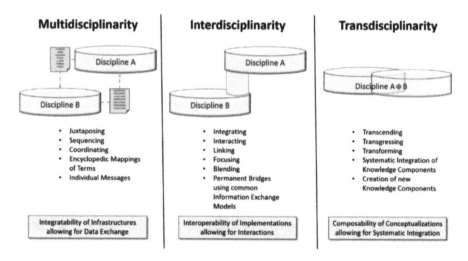

Figure 2.1. *Multi-, inter and transdisciplinary approaches*

2.3. M&S processes

The following definitions were proposed in [TOL 13a] in order to facilitate the discussion on why simulation interoperability is often harder to accomplish than interoperability in related domains. While interoperability challenges are often approached from a technical perspective of enabling data exchange, the challenge for M&S solution is more often on the conceptual perspective, as it is not sufficient to exchange data: the underlying models need to be aligned as well.

This implies that the modeling process is as important for interoperable M&S solutions as the simulation process is, if not more. Modeling is the purposeful simplification and abstraction of a perception of reality. The perception of reality is shaped by physical and cognitive – and sometimes legal and ethical – constraints. The modeler may not have full access to all data he needs (physical) or may not understand all observations immediately (cognitive). In particular, in medical cases, not all data can be obtained due to legal or ethical reasons as well: how could we justify to let patient suffer or experience harm in order to obtain data for our simulations? Furthermore, the process is driven by the modeling task – such as supporting analysis, training event or answering research questions – and the applicable modeling paradigms, which often shape the way we think about a problem and building the model. In any case, the resulting model becomes the reality of the resulting simulation. If two models are based on different theories, no data interchange can lead interoperable solutions, as the assumptions and constraints governing the solution cannot be aligned.

However, there are additional challenges to address. Simulation is an executable implementation of the model. Within this chapter, the focus lies on computer simulations. The implementation is shaped by the programming languages skills and the programming environments. Furthermore, many compromises – numeric, heuristics, computational complexity – are additional drivers for differences in the implementation. Oberkampf et al. [OBE 02] demonstrate how these lead to systemic errors and uncertainty that need to be addressed.

Not only the existence of non-compatible theories is a challenge. For decades, we know from the foundational works of Kurt Gödel and Alan Turing that all computer programs face significant epistemological constraints. Gödel's Unvollständigkeitssatz (Incompleteness Theorem) proved the general shortcomings of logic – and therefore computational logic as well – when it comes to representing truth in formal systems. Turing showed in his work on decidability that many problems cannot be solved by an algorithm. Most famous, is his proof on the halting problem that has been extended to many equivalent problems for which no algorithm can produce a solution. Both insights are valid for computer simulations as well, as they are based on algorithms and logic.

The work on reference modeling by Tolk *et al.* [TOL 13c] shows how at least the challenge of alternative theories or incompatible ontological pieces of information can be overcome. It acknowledges that in all descriptions relevant to the real-world reference of a simulation, contradictions are not only likely, but in practice generally not avoidable. The reference model collects all these pieces of information in a complete, but potentially inconsistent set of data. By creating incomplete but consistent subsets of data, conceptual models are derived from the reference model. This journal paper shows how to apply the methods of model theory to support this process. Each conceptual model can then be used to drive simulation solutions. Figure 2.2 exemplifies these ideas.

Many simulation solutions do already exist and shall be composed into a new solution. In this case, the simulation engineer has to decide, if these simulation systems actually can be composed in retrospect. In order to support the analysis, the LCIM was developed and extended to become an interoperability maturity model [TOL 13b]. Following the recommendation of [PAG 04], it distinguishes the realms of integratability of networks and physical interconnections, interoperability of simulations and implementations and the composability of concepts and models. Figure 2.3 shows the layers of the LCIM.

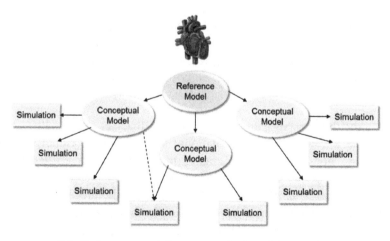

Figure 2.2. *Reference modeling, conceptual modeling and simulation*

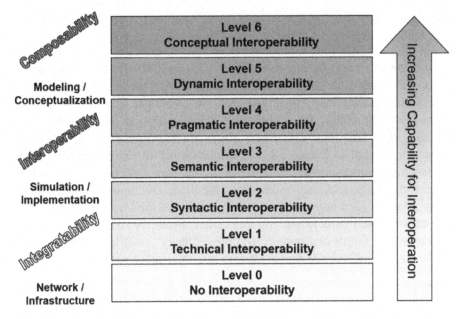

Figure 2.3. *Levels of conceptual interoperability model*

The current version of the LCIM exposes six layers of interoperation. The technical layer deals with infrastructure and network challenges, enabling systems to exchange carriers of information. The syntactic layer deals with challenges to interpret and structure the information to form symbols within protocols. The semantic layer provides a common understanding of the information exchange. On this level, the pieces of information that can be composed to objects, messages and other higher structures are identified. It represents the aligned static data. The pragmatic layer recognizes the patterns in which data are organized for the information exchange, which are in particular the inputs and outputs of procedures and methods to be called. This is the context in which data are exchanged as applicable information. These groups are often referred to as (business) objects. It represents the aligned dynamic data. The dynamic layer recognizes various system states, including the possibility for agile and adaptive systems. The same business object exchanged with different systems can trigger very different state changes. It is also possible that the same information sent to the same system at different times can trigger different responses. Finally, assumptions, constraints and simplifications need to be captured. This happens in the conceptual layer.

We can now come back to the original question of how M&S solutions can support the various disciplinary approaches, and what the implications are? In case of transdisciplinary work, we have a clear and aligned ontological foundation that allows for a common conceptualization of the application domain. M&S solutions should be supportive of all layers of the LCIM. As already addressed in Figure 2.1, the composability of the conceptualization allows for seamless system integration of the simulation solutions. When supporting interdisciplinary work, only the areas of common interest have been aligned. In these areas, however, properties and their relations and interactions are harmonized, so that interactions are possible based on interoperable implementations. Multidisciplinary solutions allow data exchange, but will require data mediation and other adjustments.

In [TOL 13a], interoperability is defined as the ability to exchange data and make use of the data within the receiving system. Composability is defined as the consistent representation of truth in all participating systems. Based on what we have seen so far, only transdisciplinary solutions will result in consistent representation of truth.

2.4. Hybrid M&S solutions

Does this mean that a support of non-aligned domains, the use of different paradigms or the application within multi- and interdisciplinary environments is not possible? Absolutely not, we just have to be aware of the underlying challenges and be careful when interpreting the results.

Powell and Mustafee [POW 14] introduced the notion of hybrid M&S studies to the community. Their view of hybrid simulation includes models that are developed by combining the methodological strengths of individual modeling techniques and paradigms. The benefit of hybrid simulation is dependent on the methodological strengths of the specific techniques and the synergy that can potentially be realized through their combined application. In other words, hybrid simulation promises to combine the best of all contributing paradigms, as long as consistency is given. Their approach also allows to conduct studies that compose various simulation system results with each other without enforcing a technical composition or federation of systems. They distinguish between hybrid simulation and a hybrid M&S study based on the techniques applied, as also the stage in which it is applied. The use of multiple M&S techniques in the model implementation is referred to as hybrid simulation, while a hybrid M&S study refers to the application of methods and techniques from alternative disciplines to one or more stages of a simulation study. Their recommended framework is depicted in Figure 2.4.

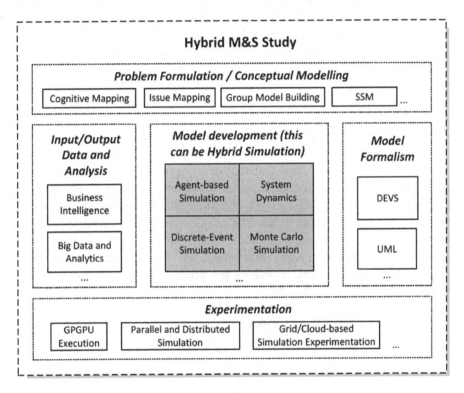

Figure 2.4. *Hybrid M&S solutions*

Hybrid M&S solution can support all stages of the various disciplinary collaboration options. They are building a perfect frame to orchestrate multi- and interdisciplinary studies and allow for tools to grow gradually with the disciplines into transdisciplinary approaches with common knowledge conceptualization and agreed reference models.

2.5. Medical simulation in support of systems biology

Biology has undergone many exciting discoveries in the last century. New technologies have allowed biologists to understand more detail than ever before. Scientists have a good understanding of the various organic systems that make up an organism such as the digestive system, the nervous system and the regenerative system. The organs making up these systems are made up of tissue that is made up of cells. Within these cells, the ribonucleic acid (RNA) and deoxyribonucleic acid (DNA) are found that produce the important proteins needed for critical life functions. While the DNA contains the genetic instructions needed, the RNA mainly conducts the work of creating, activating and deactivating certain proteins. For a long time, it was believed that once the DNA's genes are understood and mapped out, life would be better understood from the bottom-up perspective.

Noble [NOB 08] introduced a more complex view. In Figure 2.5, the interplay of various layers that make up the organism are captured following his ideas. He makes the case that a systems approach is needed to better understand the organism, as the structure is interconnected by feedbacks and connections that bridge other layers. We know that strong interrelations can be observed between the environments an organism is in, and the way DNA information is used to produce proteins. In particular when the organism gets injured, many different cells that make up the damaged tissues are collaborating via pathways to trigger the production of proteins, stop the bleeding, produce new cells, etc.

Today, on every level, simulation systems are used successfully. Examples are given by [COM 16] in various medical domains. Computational biology and bioinformatics are accepted methods in the domain of biology. Some examples for state-of-the-art text books in these domains are the texts by [BAR 15, DIS 13, LEV 13, SCH 08, VAN 11].

However, while models exist for the simulation of organs, tissue and tissue engineering and molecular and protein structure analysis, they are generally used as stand-alone tools supporting their special subdomain. For a systemic and holistic view of the organism, however, they have to be combined in support of systems biology. This requires the application of system engineering rooted principles, M&S expertise and application domain knowledge as recommended in this chapter.

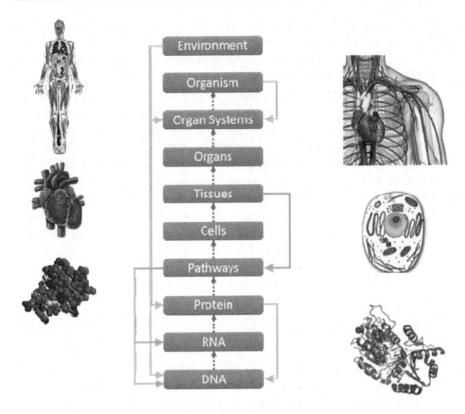

Figure 2.5. *Taxonomy of systems biology as proposed by Noble [NOB 08]*

2.6. Concluding remarks

Simulation engineers inherit a humongous responsibility, as they are likely the only professionals in the room who understand the implications of insufficiently aligned simulation applications. They have to guide the M&S solution users to better understand what this solution represents to them. It may be a metaphor to communicate ideas, or it may be seen as a subset of their perception of reality to teach apprentices and students. It can also be understood as an executable theory that can be used to gain insight and produce new knowledge.

However, if the solution is used to train people, test equipment or support researchers, the simulation engineer must know how well assumptions and constraints and underlying theories are aligned, or the resulting M&S

solution can turn into a conceptual chimera that misleads the users with results that are not based in valid theory. Winsberg [WIN 10] gives the following example to show how easy it is to compose incompatible theories into a federated simulation solution: A group of researchers is interested in how cracks evolved and move through material, such as a bridge. To address this problem, they identify three different levels of resolution. In order to understand how cracks begin, sets of atoms governed by quantum mechanics are modeled in small regions. These regions are embedded into medium-scale regions that are governed by molecular dynamics. Finally, most of the material is neither cracking nor close to a developing crack and can be modeled using continuum mechanics based on linear-elastic theory. Although these three theories cannot be mapped directly to each other, coupling heuristics can be developed. In the given example, the common expression of energy was utilized to exchange information between the regions and allow for a common model. The problem is that the three reigning theories – quantum mechanics, molecular dynamics and linear-elastic theory – cannot be applied in the same context, as they are based on contradictory assumptions and constraints. They cannot be aligned into a grand unifying theory based on transdisciplinary understanding.

The same is likely to be true in many application domains of medical simulation. It is truly a grand challenge to support systems biology, health care and related domains with simulation, but bringing them together on the levels of integration, interoperability and composability is not only an engineering challenge. It requires truly transdisciplinary approaches that not only integrate the various fields of biology and medicine, it also needs to bring in system engineers, simulation engineers, conceptual modelers and all other experts mentioned in this chapter. A reductionist approach will not be successful.

2.7. Bibliography

[BAR 15] BARNES D.J., CHU D., *Guide to Simulation and Modeling for Biosciences*, 2nd ed., Springer, London, 2015.

[COM 16] COMBS C.D., SOKOLOWSKI J.A., BANKS C.M., *The Digital Patient: Advancing Healthcare Research and Education*, John Wiley & Sons., Hoboken, NJ, 2016.

[DIS 13] DISTEFANO III J., *Dynamic Systems Biology Modeling and Simulation*, Academic Press/Elsevier, Amsterdam, 2013.

[LEV 13] LEVINE A.I., DEMARIA Jr. S., SCHWARTZ A.D. *et al.*, *The Comprehensive Textbook of Healthcare Simulation*, Springer, New York, 2013.

[NOB 08] NOBLE D., *The Music of Life: Biology Beyond Genes*, Oxford University Press, UK, 2008.

[OBE 02] OBERKAMPF W.L., DELAND S.M., RUTHERFORD B.M. *et al.*, "Error and uncertainty in modeling and simulation", *Reliability Engineering & System Safety* vol. 75, no. 3, pp. 333–357, 2002.

[PAG 04] PAGE E.H., BRIGGS R., TUFAROLO J.A., "Toward a family of maturity models for the simulation interconnection problem", *Proceedings of the Spring Simulation Interoperability Workshop*, Paper 04S-SIW-145, SISO, Orlando, 2004.

[POW 14] POWELL J., MUSTAFEE N., "Soft OR approaches in problem formulations stage of a hybrid M&S study", *Proceedings of the Winter Simulation Conference*, IEEE Press, Piscataway, pp. 1664–1675, 2014.

[SCH 08] SCHWARTZ R., *Biological Modeling and Simulation: A Survey of Practical Models, Algorithms, and Numerical Methods*, MIT Press, Cambridge, 2008.

[STO 01] STOCK P., BURTON R.J.F., "Defining terms for integrated (multi-inter-trans-disciplinary) sustainability research", *Sustainability*, vol. 3, pp. 1090–1113, 2001.

[TOL 13a] TOLK A., "Interoperability, composability, and their implications for distributed simulation – towards mathematical foundations of simulation interoperability", *Proceedings of the DS-RT Conference*, IEEE Press, Piscataway, pp. 3–9, 2013.

[TOL 13b] TOLK A., BAIR L.J., DIALLO S.Y., "Supporting network enabled capability by extending the levels of conceptual interoperability model to an interoperability maturity model", *Journal of Defense Modeling and Simulation: Applications, Methodology, Technology*, vol. 10, no. 2, pp. 145–160, 2013.

[TOL 13c] TOLK A., DIALLO S.Y., PADILLA J.J. *et al.*, "Reference modelling in support of M&S – foundations and applications", *Journal of Simulation*, vol. 7, no.2, pp. 69–82, 2013.

[VAN 11] VAN MEURS W., *Modeling and Simulation in Biomedical Engineering: Applications in Cardiorespiratory Physiology*, McGraw Hill, New York, 2011.

[WIN 10] WINSBERG E., *Science in the Age of Computer Simulation*, University of Chicago Press, 2010.

3

Heterogeneous Computing: An Emerging Paradigm of Embedded Systems Design

Heterogeneous computing and systems are a reality today and are an emerging paradigm of embedded system design due to their energy efficiency. Heterogeneous systems provide the best performance/power efficiency trade-offs and are the natural choice for embedded systems. In addition, the heterogeneous cores increase performance by dividing the work among well-matched cores. These systems generally use irregular memory and irregular interconnection networks that also save power by reducing the loads in the whole network. Understanding the software and hardware building blocks and the computation power of individual components in these complex systems is necessary for designing power, performance and cost-efficient systems. This chapter describes in detail the architectures and functions of the main building blocks that are used to build complex heterogeneous computing systems.

3.1. Introduction

With the increasing processing power demands of embedded applications and technology advances, heterogeneous Multicore Systems on Chip (Mcsocs) have become prevalent in embedded systems. A typical MCSoC includes several optimized components integrated together to execute a specific application. Applications range from digital cameras, cellular phones, set-top boxes, PDAs to biomedical and military instruments.

Chapter written by Abderazak BEN ABDALLAH.

Different functions in these embedded MCSoCs are typically implemented with software running on an RISC, digital signal processors (DSPs), or with dedicated hardware Intellectual Property (IP) blocks. These blocks are available from vendors as hard or soft cores. We will discuss later in this chapter how to select these IP cores to build power- and performance-efficient multicore systems. The availability of various IP cores with different performance and complexity from many existing providers makes the selection more difficult. In addition, selecting suitable cores also depends on the available power, area and cost budgets. Therefore, a designer must be careful and aware about all these factors before even thinking about higher level organization of the target system.

Organization of an MCSoC architecture means that the software and hardware relationships between different IP blocks (including on-chip/off-chip memory) and the interconnection network, which links these IP cores together in an efficient manner, are such that several design and performance constraints are satisfied. The hardware and software design team should also be aware about the real-time performance requirement of the system being designed. This is very important because generally a real-time system has more design constraints than a regular multicore system. Consequently, the design of real-time MCSoCs is much more complex than the design of general embedded systems.

Modern MCSoC organization guidelines include separation between computation and communication, and between functions and architectures. The applications that need to run on these MCSoCs have become increasingly complex and have very strict power and performance requirements. Thus, achieving a satisfactory design quality under these circumstances is only possible when both communication and computation refinements are performed efficiently.

MCSoCs can be homogeneous or heterogeneous systems. The organization of each category is of course different. The main difference is in the type and computation power of integrated IP cores. Figure 3.1 shows a general view of a typical modern MCSoC organization and Figure 3.2 shows an example of an embedded multicore system of a typical digital camera device. The reader should be also aware that a number of programmable MCSoC platforms are now commercially available, such as Cell from IBM, Nomadik from STMicroelectronics and many others.

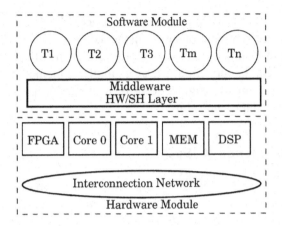

Figure 3.1. *General organization view of a modern typical MCSoC*

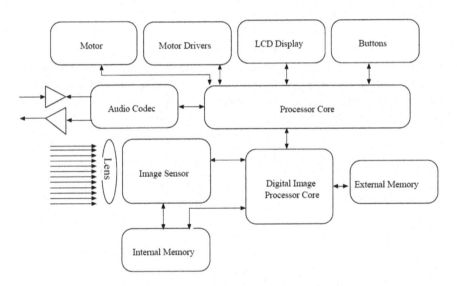

Figure 3.2. *Example of an embedded multicore system for a typical digital still camera*

To let the reader first get the "big picture" of such MCSoC systems, we will explain in the next part of this section the two main MCSoC categories – homogeneous and heterogeneous. In this chapter, we only focus on the main building blocks of MCSoC systems. The system, which we assume here, is generic and not restricted to a specific kind of embedded application. The reason is that most building blocks, such as on-chip memory, microprocessor(s), peripheral interfaces, Input/Output (I/O) logic control, data converters and other components are found in most embedded applications. For example, the single chip phone, which has been introduced by several semiconductor vendors, is an example; it includes a modem, radio transceiver, a multimedia engine, security features and power management functionality all on the same chip.

3.1.1. *Heterogeneous MCSoC*

A heterogeneous MCSoC is a single chip that combines different cores having different instruction set architectures and computing power with a sophisticated network or simple shared medium to efficiently link all components together.

Application designers or high-level compilers can choose the most efficient IP cores for the type of processing needed for a given application task. The main motivation behind these systems is the fact that many applications, such as MPEG-2 encoder (see Figure 3.3), have more than one algorithm during their execution life. This means that a given application has different operations, different memory access patterns and different communication bandwidths at different execution periods.

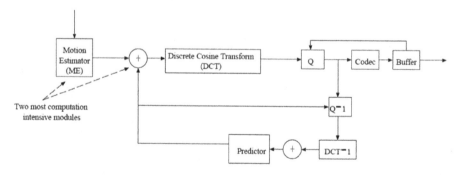

Figure 3.3. *Example of MPEG-2 encoder for a heterogeneous MCSoC system*

Another example is in advanced safety automobile devices, where multiple applications, consisting of several tasks, are executed simultaneously. Each task, invoked by applications, such as image processing, recognition, control or measurement, is assigned to a single processor core. Heterogeneous MCSoCs provide the best performance/

power efficiency trade-offs and are the natural choice for embedded systems. The heterogeneous cores increase performance by dividing the work among well-matched cores. This requires many central processing unit (CPU) cores for general-purpose processing as well as several Single Instruction Multiple Data (SIMD) processor cores to accelerate specific performance-critical processing. The heterogeneous SoC can save energy at almost all levels (device, circuit and logic) of abstraction. In addition, these systems generally use irregular memory and irregular interconnection networks that also save power by reducing the loads in the whole network.

Figure 3.4 shows an example of a heterogeneous MCSoC organization. The above system integrates several typical cores (RISC, accelerators, Very Long Instruction Word (VLIW), SIMD, etc.), which are found in most modern heterogeneous MCSoC systems. The different cores are generally connected to a common pipelined bus (single or multilayer) with a cache coherence mechanism (discussed later), such as the well-known Modified, Exclusive, Shared or Invalid (MESI) protocol [PAP 84]. The embedded L2 cache, internal I/O and synchronous dynamic random access memory (SDRAM) are all connected to the bus. The SIMD core is generally a highly specialized parallel processor and is used to process large amount of data, such as images. Additionally, a cache memory is shared by the CPU cores to reduce internal bus traffic and access to the main slow DRAM memory.

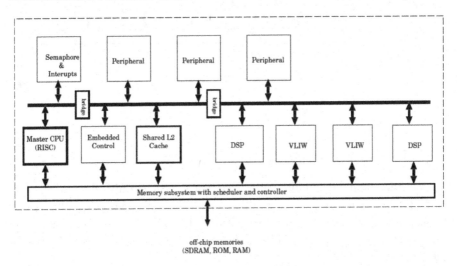

Figure 3.4. *Heterogeneous MCSoC organization example*

3.1.2. *Homogeneous MCSoC*

An alternative to the previously discussed system is called homogeneous MCSoC. This system is typically built with the same programmable building blocks instantiated several times. This alternative model is often referred to in the literature as the parallel architecture model. Parallel architectures have been particularly studied in computer science and engineering over the past 40 years. Nowadays, there is a growing interest in such approaches in embedded systems. Figure 3.5 illustrates an example of a typical homogeneous MCSoC organization example. The basic principle of an architecture that exhibits parallel processing capabilities relies on increasing the number of physical resources in order to divide the execution time of each resource.

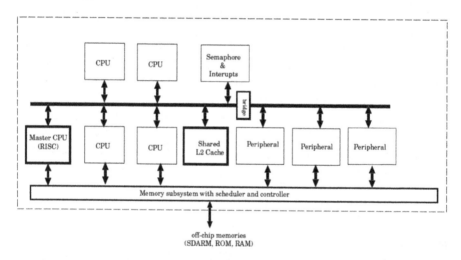

Figure 3.5. *Homogeneous MCSoC organization example*

3.1.3. *Multicore SoC applications*

As with general architectures, MCSoCs are mainly driven by the performance requirements of applications. Therefore, knowing the target application(s) of the system before starting the design is important not only for the selection of appropriate PEs, but also for reducing the overall cost of the system.

There are four well-known applications for MCSoC systems: (1) wireless, (2) network, (3) multimedia and (4) mobile applications. The remainder of this section describes these applications and gives some examples of MCSoCs designed for these applications.

– *Wireless applications*: In this class of applications, MCSoCs are mainly used as wireless base stations (i.e. Luceny Daytona [KNO 00]) in which identical signal processing is performed on a number of data channels. Daytona is a homogeneous system with four SPARC V8 CPU cores attached to a high-speed split transaction. Each CPU has an 8-KB 16-bank cache and each bank can be configured as instruction cache, data cache or Scratchpad. The cores share a common address space (see Figure 3.6).

– *Network applications*: In this second class, an MCSoC can be used as a network processor for packet processing in off-chip networks. The C-5 processor is an example of a network processor [CPO 01]. In this system, packets are handled by channel cores that are grouped into four clusters of four units each. The traffic of all cores is handled by three buses. In addition to the channel cores, there are also several specialized cores. The executive processor core is an RISC architecture.

– *Multimedia applications*: Multimedia applications implemented on consumer electronics devices span a vast range of functionality from audio decoders such as MP3 via video decoders such as H.264 up to advanced picture quality processing such as frame rate upconversion and Motion Accurate Picture Processing. Hybrid TV solutions are a very good example because they are capable of executing virtually any of these multimedia applications.

– *Mobile applications*: The fourth class of MCSoCs application is in the mobile cell phone. Earlier cell phone processors performed base-band operations, including both communication and multimedia operations. As an example, the Texas Instruments' OMAP architecture has several implementations. The OMAP 5912 has two CPU cores: an ARM9 and a TMS320C55x DSP. The ARM core acts as a master and the DSP core acts as a slave that performs signal processing operations. Another example was implemented by STMicroelectronics and is called Nomadik [STM 05]. It uses an ARM926EJ as its host processor. The ARM926EJ-S processor core runs at up to 350 MHz in 130 nm CMOS process and up to 500 MHz in 90 nm CMOS. The core includes onboard cache, Java acceleration in its hardware and strong real-time debug support. Namdik systems are aimed at

2.5G and 3G mobile phones, personal digital assistants and other portable wireless products with multimedia capability.

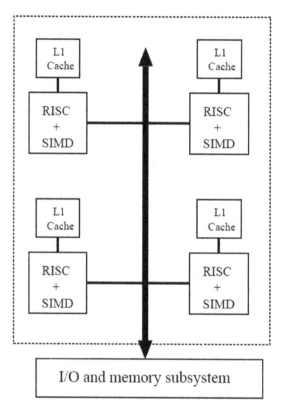

Figure 3.6. *Example of MCSoC application in wireless communication: Lucent Daytona MCSoC*

3.1.4. *Applications mapping*

As discussed above, today's MCSoC architectures are composed of commercially available off-the-shelf IP blocks. Ultimately, we would like to design a generic heterogeneous MCSoC architecture that is flexible enough to run different applications. However, mapping an application to such heterogeneous SoC is more difficult compared to mapping to a homogeneous one. Today, general practice is to map applications to the architecture at design-time or run-time. Run-time mapping offers a number of advantages over design time mapping. It mainly offers the following possibilities:

– to avoid defective parts of an SoC. Larger chip area means lower yield. The yield can be improved when the mapper is able to avoid faulty parts of the chip. Also aging can lead to faulty parts that are unforeseeable at design-time;

– to adapt to the available resources. The available resources are only known to the mapping algorithm at run-time. In addition, the available resources may vary over time, for example, due to applications running simultaneously or adaptation of algorithms to the environment;

– to enable upgrades of the system.

The objective of the run-time mapping is to determine at run-time a near-optimal mapping of the application to the architecture using the library of process implementations and the current status of the system.

The mapping of the functional subsystems onto SoC hardware resources may be based on a number of considerations:

– *Support*: Support of industry standards. This is very important for processor cores that are programmed by the designers. Generally, industry standard CPU cores have extensive tool chain and library support that eases the application design and debug.

– *Performance:* Computationally intensive algorithms such as HD H.264 decoder cannot be implemented effectively on a general purpose processor because of the computational complexity. Instead, a function specific HW core is needed.

– *Flexibility*: Evolving standards require flexibility in implementations so that new codecs can be added without the need for a new SoC. This reduces cost and time.

– *Re-usability:* Implementation, integration and verification are time-consuming tasks and sometimes it is appropriate not to implement a function on the most optimum SoC HW resource in order to make it reusable in future SoCs.

3.2. MCSoC building blocks

A typical MCSoC is composed of several components: memories, processing elements, input/output subsystem and communication subsystem. In most of these MCSoC systems, the cores have separate L1 caches, but share a L2 cache, memory subsystem, interrupt subsystem and peripherals. Figure 3.7 illustrates a simplified block diagram of a typical MCSoC architecture having different building blocks.

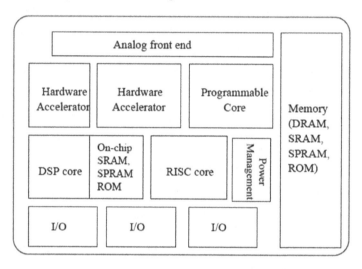

Figure 3.7. *Simplified view of a typical MCSoC architecture with different core and memory types*

Figure 3.8 shows a general view of a state of the art MCSoC system based on network-on-chip (NoC) interconnection. In NoC interconnection, PEs communicate with each other using packets and not messages as with shared bus.

Although systems that are built with the NoC approach are scalable and power efficient, the design of such systems is not easy when compared with the design of systems based on shared buses. The reason for such complexity is that the designer must care not only about the computational (PEs) part, but they must also care about the communication part (how to route packets). In other words, they must carefully select appropriate topology, routing scheme, control flow and network interface (NI). Among these blocks, the

NI is a complex and very important component that must be carefully designed.

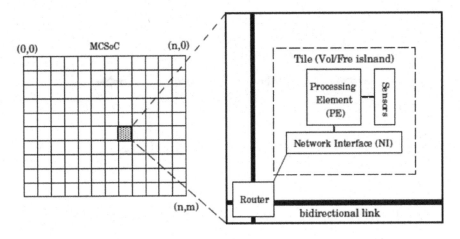

Figure 3.8. *State of the art MCSoC architecture based on network-on-chip paradigm*

The PEs type and computation power depends on the application context and requirements. As we explained in section 3.1, we distinguish two types of architectures: (1) heterogeneous MCSoCs and (2) homogeneous MCSoCs. Heterogeneous systems are composed of different IPs, such as processors, memories, accelerators and peripherals. A homogeneous system is a system where the same tile is instantiated several times. Beyond its hardware architecture, MCSoC generally runs a set of software applications divided into tasks and an operating system devoted to manage both hardware and software through a middle-ware layer. Figure 1.1 shows a general view of an MCSoC and the interfacing between the software and hardware modules.

3.2.1. *Processor core*

The type and the computation power of the processor core, which is embedded in a given MCSoC, depends on the target application and whether the core is used for control purposes (master) or computation purposes (slave). Figure 3.9 shows the pipeline stages of a typical RISC processor core. The stages are as follows: fetch, decode, execute, memory access and write-back.

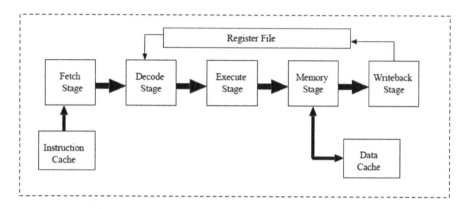

Figure 3.9. *Typical five pipeline stages of an RISC processor core*

3.2.2. *Memory*

In an MCSoC, several masters communicate with a single or at most a few dynamic RAM (DRAM) memory slaves. The DRAM memory subsystem consists of a memory scheduler, a memory the controller and the DRAM memory. The scheduler arbitrates between multiple requests, whereas the controller takes care of bit-level protocol of the DRAM device and activates, refreshes, etc. In some designs, a sophisticated scheduler reorders the requests such that the DRAM's efficiency is maximized by means of high page hit rate, and low Read-Write direction turnaround. Figure 3.10 shows an example of an MCSoC based on a network-on-chip interconnection network with a single external DRAM memory. In this example, the additional latency added by the router may become a real problem if the memory is highly utilized. That is, for example, when there is high traffic between the external DRAM and one or more PEs within the system. Such a traffic scenario is called a traffic hot-spot, which affects large portions of the network because blocked traffic reserves many routers and links.

In addition, the requirement to refresh the DRAM at some regular periods reduces the total achievable bandwidth. Moreover, the efficiency is dependent upon the type of transactions and the address patterns that are presented to the DRAM.

3.2.3. Cache

Most multicore systems today have one or two levels of dedicated private caches, backed up with a shared last level cache (LLC). The performance and power consumption of an MCSoC is strongly dependent on the performance of the LLC because the LLC can help reduce off-chip memory traffic and contention for memory bandwidth. Figure 3.11 shows three levels of caches in a single node of a typical MCSoC. Cache is efficient because of a program property called *Locality*. The locality says that if a program accesses a particular memory address, it is likely that the next few accesses will be to nearby addresses (spatial locality), and also that the same address is likely to be accessed again within a short time (temporal locality). This is true for instruction fetches, and also for data reads and writes.

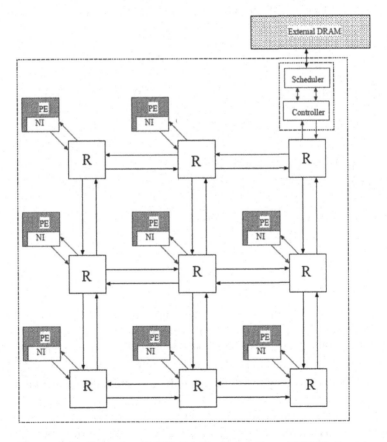

Figure 3.10. *Example of MCSoC with single external DRAM memory*

System designer can take advantage of the locality of references to create a hierarchical memory with multiple levels of memory of different speeds and sizes. At the top of this hierarchy, we have a fast, but small memory, which is directly connected to the processor core. The memory size increases as we move to lower levels of the hierarchy further away from the processor core. Howerer, the speed drops as we move to lower levels of the hierarchy further away from the processor core.

The minimum amount of data transferred between two adjacent memory levels is called a block or line. Although this could be as small as one word, the spatial locality principle suggests that a designer should design caches with larger blocks. If the data requested by a given core are found at a memory level, we say that we have a *hit* at that level. If not, we have a *miss* and the request is sent to the next level down and the block containing the requested data is copied at this level when the data are found. The reason for copying the missed block containing the requested data to the cache is to ensure that the next time these (or nearby) data are accessed, there will be a hit at this level. The memory system in an MCSoC architecture generally consists of a four-level hierarchy: Registers, Scratchpad, cache and main memory.

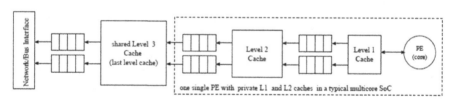

Figure 3.11. *Cache organization in a single node of a typical MCSoC*

3.2.3.1. Communication protocols

For a given number of cores, the most appropriate interconnection network depends on a combination of factors including area/power, budget, technology, performance objectives and bandwidth requirements. We have to note here that unlike conventional multiprocessors, performance is not necessarily maximized by the highest bandwidth interconnect available.

The traditional form of functional interconnect between different cores in a simple SoC is the on-chip bus, which is an array of wires with multiple writers under a mutual-exclusion control scheme. Buses are very simple to design and permit the implementation of efficient hardware mechanisms to enforce cache consistency. In addition, bus-based systems have fair throughput as long as the system is small and there are not too many masters that initiate data transfers. This is the case with single-core SoC devices, where typically only the core and some advanced peripherals can function as bus masters. Typically, IPs are connected to the bus via standardized protocols, such as Advanced extensible Interface (AXI), Device Transaction Level (DTL) and Open Core Protocol (OCP).

By using large caches, it is possible to reduce the bus traffic produced by each core, thus allowing systems with greater numbers of cores to be built. Unfortunately, capacitive loading on the bus increases as the number of cores is increased. This effect increases the minimum time required for a bus operation; thus reducing the maximum bus bandwidth.

Multibus solutions have provided a temporary solution for small-scale systems. However, for large-scale systems a better solution is still needed. NoC is the promising interconnection paradigm for these complex multi- and many-core SoCs. Figure 3.12 shows the evolution chart of on-chip communication interconnects for single and MCSoCs.

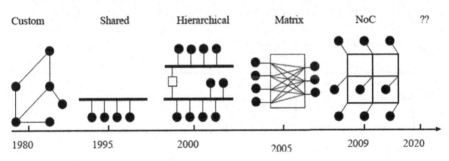

Figure 3.12. *Evolution of on-chip communication interconnect*

3.2.3.2. Packet-switched interconnect

The PEs integrated within modern and future MCSoC are (will be) mostly interconnected by a packet-switched network also called NoC [BEN 06]. NoC consists of a network of shared communication links and routers, which connect to the various cores through NIs. These NIs convert between the internal NoC protocol on one side and the core's protocol on the other.

For reasons of compatibility and reuse, the latter is typically one of the standardized bus protocols such as AXI, DTL and OCP (see Figure 3.13).

The NI module decouples computation from communication functions. Routers are in charge of routing and arbitrate the date between the source and destination PEs through links.

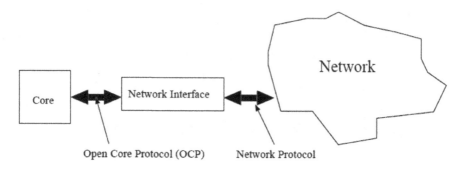

Figure 3.13. *Open Core Protocol (OCP) and Network Protocol (NP) interfacing*

Several network topologies have been studied. The NoCs facilitate the design of Globally Asynchronous Locally Synchronous property by implementing asynchronous–synchronous interfaces in the NIs. Figure 3.14 shows an example of NoC operation.

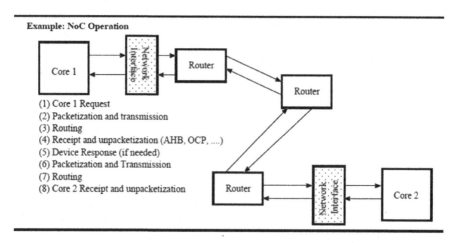

Figure 3.14. *NoC operation*

3.2.4. IP cores

An IP core is a block of logic or a software library that we use to design an SoC based on single or multicore. These software and hardware IPs are designed and highly optimized in advance (time to market consideration) by specialized companies and are ready to be integrated with our new design. For example, we may buy a software library to perform some complex graphic operations and integrate that library with our existing code. We may also obtain the above code freely from an open-source site online. Universal Asynchronous Receiver/Transmitter, CPUs, Ethernet controllers and PCI interfaces are all examples of hardware IP cores.

As essential elements of design reuse, IP cores are part of the growing electronic design automation industry trend toward repeated use of previously designed components. Ideally, an IP core should be entirely portable. This means the core must be able to easily be integrated (plug-and-play style) into any vendor technology or design methodology. Of course, there are some IPs that are not standard and may need some kind of interface (called wrapper) before integrating it into a design. IP cores fall into one of two main categories, i.e. soft cores and hard cores:

1) Soft IP core: Soft IP cores refer to circuits that are available at a higher level of abstraction such as register-transfer level (RTL). These types of cores can be customized by the user for specific applications.

2) Hard IP Core: A hard IP core is one where the circuit is available at a lower level of abstraction such as the layout level. For this type of core, it is impossible to customize it to suit the requirements of the embedded system. As a result, there are limited opportunities in optimizing the cost functions by modifying the hard IP.

A good IP core should be configurable so that it can meet the needs of many different designs. It also should have a standard interface so that it can be integrated easily. Finally, a good IP core should come in the form of complete sets of deliverables: synthesizable RTL, complete test benches, synthesis scripts and documentation. The example shown in Figure 3.15 is for a hardware IP core from Altera FPGA provider [ALT 12].

Example: Altera Intellectual Property

The Altera IP core site (http://www.altera.com/products/ip/ip-index.jsp)
Altera IP site provides access to a wide variety of IP blocks of different
size and complexity:

- basic arithmetic blocks to transceivers,
- memory controllers,
- microprocessors,
- signal processing, and
- protocol interfaces

Figure 3.15. *Intellectual property example*

3.2.5. IP cores with multiple clock domains

The IP cores integrated within a given MCSoC may work at different
clock rates. For example, some SoC may have more than three clock
domains. In addition, many embedded cores operate internally using
multiple frequencies. Figure 3.16 shows a simple design that comprises three
cores with three different physical clocks. In this example, Core 2 consists of
three modules operating at different frequencies (f1, f2 and f3). A physical
clock is a chip-level clock; for example, it can come from an oscillator or a
phase locked loop (PILL). All the internal clocks generated from the same
physical clock are considered to be part of the same physical clock domain.

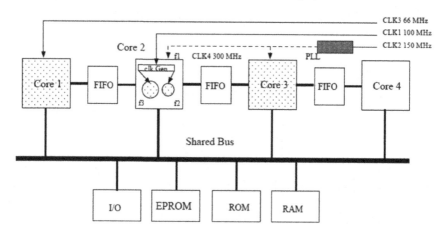

Figure 3.16. *Three clock domains MCSoC*

In an MCSoC system, the multifrequency blocks communicate with each other through synchronization logic and/or First In First Out (FIFO) memory blocks. Such design has the advantage of low power and low silicon area. However, the main design difficulties with multifrequency embedded cores are the clock skew and synchronization problems.

3.2.6. Selection of IP cores

This section investigates the classification and selection of processor cores and considers the MCSoC infrastructure that allows an efficient mix of different types of cores and function-specific hardware cores to access shared resources in the SoC. Selection of appropriate IP cores depends on the application mapping output. Depending on the target application, mapping of the functional subsystems to an MCSoC hardware resource generally involves the following cores:

– *Host CPU*: The host CPU is generally an industry standard core such as MIPS and ARM CPUs. Typically, these cores have a large application code and thus need to access code and data in an external SDRAM memory.

– *VLIW processor*: Generally, this core provides scalability and processing power. This processor core exploits fine-grained data parallelism. Code and data segments are typically large, so the VLIW processor core also needs access to SDRAM.

– *Embedded control CPU*: Small- to medium-sized code bases often use, for architectural and commercial reasons, processor cores from the same processor provider as the host CPU. For architectural consistency, such cores are connected to the same bus structures as the host CPU or VLIW processor cores.

– *Fixed point DSP*: Generally, deeply embedded into the MCSoC architecture. Often, DSP cores are connected into the SoC infrastructure via HW semaphore mechanisms.

– *Function-specific HW core*: Massively parallel computation core that makes use of fine-grained parallelism as well as coarser parallelism and typically processes large data sets. Some cores are connected to external real-time interfaces, and therefore need real-time performance.

As an example of mapping a given application to different cores within an MCSoC system, consider an example of an MPEG-2 decoder application that consists of a baseline unit, a motion compensation (MC) unit, a recovery unit and the associated buffers. The baseline unit consists of a variable length decoder, an   inverse quantization/inverse zigzag module, inverse discrete cosine transform modules and the buffer. Figure 3.17 shows this application running on a multicore system with two or three cores.

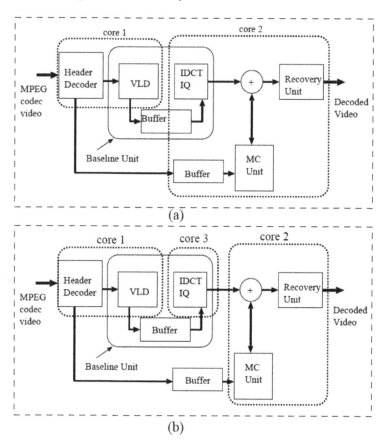

Figure 3.17. *Example of mapping of an MPEG-2 decoder: a) using two cores and b) using three cores*

3.3. MCSoC memory hierarchy

The memory architecture of an embedded MCSoC strongly influences the area, power and performance of the entire system. In these systems, more on-chip silicon is devoted to memory than to anything else on the chip. This requires special attention that must be dedicated to the on-chip memory organization.

The memory organization of embedded MCSoC systems varies widely from one to another, depending on the application and market segment for which the SoC is targeted. Broadly speaking, program memories for MCSoCs are classified into (1) primary memory and (2) secondary memory.

The primary memory is the memory that is addressed by core(s) and holds the current data set that is being processed as well as the program (text) code. This memory may consist of main memory typically implemented in DRAM technology, and a hierarchy of smaller and faster caches (static random access memory [SRAMs]) or Scratchpad memories (SPRAMs) that hold the copies of some of the data from the main memory.

The secondary memory may also be used for long-term storage. Embedded MCSoC systems often include flash memory as the secondary storage, e.g. for storing pictures in a digital camera.

In the remaining part of this section, we will discuss in a fair amount of detail the many alternatives for on-chip and off-chip memory usage that SoC designers must understand.

3.3.1. Types of on-chip memory

There are three broad categories of on-chip memories that a system designer can use. The first type is called SRAM. This is quite a well-known memory architecture and is found in almost every type of computer and not only in embedded multicore systems. SRAM is very common in SoC designs because it is fast and is built from the same transistors used to build all of the logic on the SoC, so no process changes are required. Furthermore, due to its good characteristics (mainly speed), SRAMs are generally used for caches to solve the processor-memory speed mismatches.

Most SRAM bit cells require at least four transistors and some require as many as 10; so on-chip DRAM is becoming increasingly popular. DRAM stores bits as capacitive charge, so each DRAM bit cell requires only one transistor and a capacitor. DRAM's main advantage is density. But, DRAM is slower than SRAM and has some particular requirements that affect system design such as the need for periodic refresh. Furthermore, the capacitors in the DRAM bit cells require specialized processing, which increases die cost. This is of course not a good situation for strictly cost constrained embedded MCSoC systems.

Every SoC needs memory that remembers code and data even when the power is off. Thus, the cheapest and least flexible memory is ROM and so is our second type of memory in this discussion. ROMs are not flexible since their contents cannot be changed after the system is fabricated. Fortunately, Erasable Programmable Read Only Memory (EPROM) and flash memory are good alternatives. Figure 3.18 illustrates a simplified view of an MCSoC architecture with different cores and memory types.

A given memory bank can be organized as a single-access RAM or a dual-access RAM to provide single or dual access to the memory bank in a single cycle. Also, the on-chip memory banks can be of different sizes.

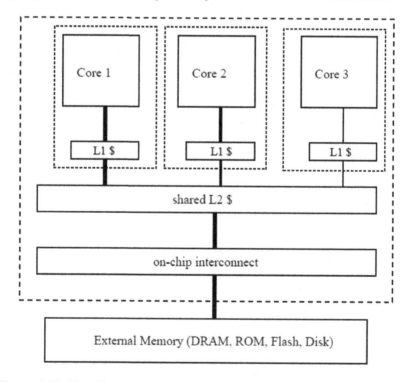

Figure 3.18. *Simplified view of an MCSoC architecture having different memories*

The good thing about smaller banks is that they consume less power per access than the larger memories. Embedded multicore systems may also be interfaced to off-chip memory, which can include SRAM and DRAM. If the system is targeted for low to medium complexity embedded applications, purely SPRAM-based on-chip organization is recommended. FIFO memories can also be used for intercore communication inside the MCSoC chip as shown in Figure 3.19.

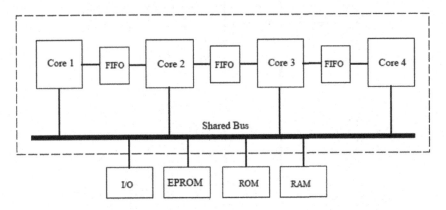

Figure 3.19. *Example of four cores communicating via FIFOs*

3.3.2. Scratchpad memory

Scratchpad memory (SPRAM) is a high-speed internal memory directly connected to the CPU core and used for temporary storage to hold very small items of data for rapid retrieval. Scratchpads are employed for simplification of caching logic and to guarantee a unit can work without main memory contention in a system employing multiple cores, especially in embedded MCSoC systems. They are suited to storing temporary results.

While a cache memory uses a complex hardware controller to decide which data to keep in cache memories (L1 or L2) and which data to prefetch, the SPRAM approach does not require any hardware support in addition to the memory itself, but requires software to take control of all data transfers to and from Scratchpad memories. It is therefore the responsibility of the programmer to identify data sections that should be placed in SPRAM or place code in the program to appropriately move data from on-chip memory to SPRAM. For this reason, SPRAMs are sometimes called "software controlled caches". Figure 3.20 illustrates the memory subsystem architecture with two SPRAMs (levels 1 and 2).

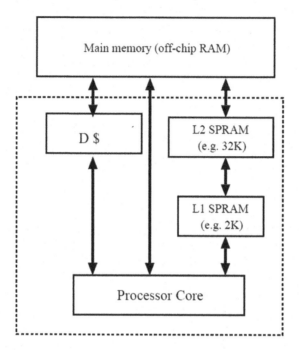

Figure 3.20. *MCSoC memory subsystem with SPRAM (only interconnection for one node is shown for simplicity)*

3.3.3. Off-chip memory

When embedded system designers need a large amount of RAM storage, then off-chip double-data-rate (DDR) SDRAM is likely to be the good choice. Even if an embedded design only requires a small fraction of the capacity of a DDR memory chip or module, it may still be more economical to pay for the excess capacity because the system price will still be lower.

Adding a DDR memory port to an MCSoC design creates the need for an on-chip DDR memory controller. In the same way, system design considerations may make it more desirable to have non-volatile memory reside off-chip. Again, this option is adopted when large non-volatile memory is needed or when the manufacturing costs needed to add Electrically Erasable Programmable Read Only Memory (EEPROM) to the

MCSoC are expensive due to limited available budget. In this case, the hardware design team should add a Flash memory controller, which of course will add some extra hardware and cost to the system.

3.3.4. *Memory power reduction in SoC designs*

Due to recent increases in Very Large Scale Integration (VLSI) density, SoC designers have exploited the additional silicon available on chips to integrate embedded memories such as SPRAMs, FIFOs and caches to store data for the large number of cores.

Since these embedded memories are implemented inside the chip, the communication latency is low or even negligible. Thus, they allow for significantly better system performance and lower power compared to a solution where off-chip memories are used.

It was found by several researchers that the memory subsystem accounts for up to 50–70% of the total power consumption of the system [ITR 05]. This reflects the importance of limiting the energy consumption of memory subsystems. One possible architectural approach for memory energy reduction is the replacement of a traditional cache-based memory subsystem with customized SPRAM-based one.

The energy savings from this solution come from the fact that SPRAM consumes less energy per access than a cache due to the absence of additional hardware (e.g. tag memory) present in a cache.

With more transistors becoming available on chip, the percentage of area taken by memory is increasing. In addition to the power projection, the [ITR 03] report projects that in 2012, memory will occupy about 90% of a chip. This means that only about 10% will be left for the processor's computing blocks. Figure 3.21 shows the projection of memory/logic composition of a power-constrained SoC chips.

As we mentioned earlier, most memories embedded in MCSoCs use SRAM technology. The key sources of power consumption in such memories are:

– static or leakage power dissipated by the logic in the periphery and memory array;

– dynamic or switching power dissipated when read or write operations are performed.

The dynamic power consumed by a memory when a read or write operation occurs can be divided into the power consumed by the following components:

– toggling of the clock network;

– registers for data/address latching on memory I/Os;

– bit-lines in the memory array;

– peripheral logic to decode the address;

– core memory cells changing state.

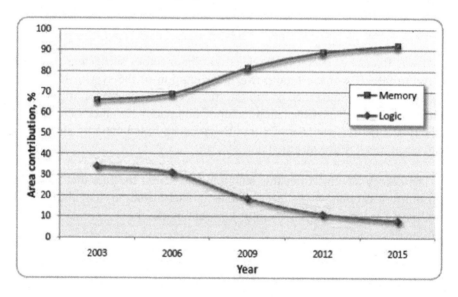

Figure 3.21. *Projection of memory/logic composition of power-constrained SoC chips [ITR 03]*

3.4. Memory consistency in multicore systems

In the traditional Von Neumann machines, instructions appear to execute in the order specified by the programmer or compiler regardless of whether the implementation of the machine actually executes them in a different order. For example, a load instruction should return the last value written to the memory location. Likewise, a store instruction to a memory location determines the value of the next load. All sequential programs assume this strict rule when they are executed on a uniprocessor.

Multithreaded programs running on multicore systems complicate both the programming model and the implementation to enforce a given model. More precisely, the value returned by a given load is not clear because the most recent store instruction may have occurred on a different core. Thus, system designers generally define memory consistency models to specify how a processor core can observe memory accesses from other cores in the same system. Serial consistency is a model defined such that the result of any execution is the same as if the operations of all processor cores were executed in a serial order, and the operations of each individual core behave in this sequence in the order specified by its program. The addition of cache memories to these systems affects how such consistency is implemented.

A cache memory allows processor speed to increase at a greater rate than the main memory speed by exploiting what is known as "time" and "space" localities.

The process of connecting memory locations with cache lines is called "mapping". Since cache is smaller than the main memory, the same cache lines are shared for different memory locations. Each cache line has a record of the memory address called tag. This tag is used to track which area of memory is stored in a particular cache line.

The way these tags are mapped to cache lines can have a beneficial effect on the way a program runs. Caches can be organized in one of several ways: direct mapped, fully associative and set associative. Figure 3.22 shows an example of direct-mapped cache organization. Cache operations are mainly done in hardware and their operation is all hardware-based and automatic from a programmer's point of view. In other words, details of the cache hierarchy does not affect the instruction set architecture of the processor. While caches do not present a real problem in a uniprocessor system, they considerably complicate memory consistency for systems designed with multi- and many-cores. This problem is known in the literature as *cache coherence* problem.

3.4.1. *Cache coherence problem*

In a single-core system, the coherence problem appears when an I/O peripheral bypasses the cache on the system bus and flows directly to and from the main memory (DRAM). This problem can easily be solved by software (compiler) because the single thread context imposes a well-defined thread order and the software is always informed on each trap and interrupt caused by a given I/O. The compiler then tags data as cacheable and non-cacheable. Only read-only data are considered cacheable and put in private cache. All other data are non-cacheable and can be put in a global cache, if available.

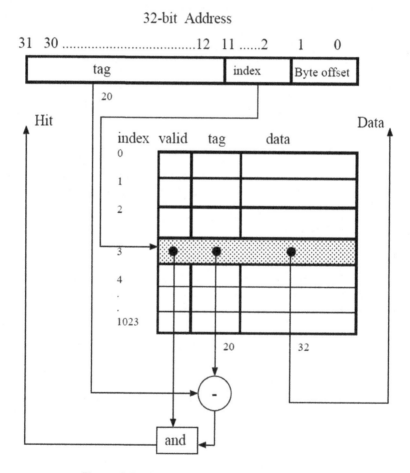

Figure 3.22. *Direct-mapped cache organization*

In multicore-based systems, things are quite different and more serious because it is difficult to keep a record on the order of instructions in different threads running simultaneously and in different processor cores.

This "coherence" problem comes from the multiple copies of the same memory location, not only in the cache hierarchy, but also in more low-level hardware buffers for memory accesses inside the processor core. The coherence problem here is more difficult to solve than in single core systems because the software is not always informed and on-chip communication patterns are not clearly seen by the system's software.

Figure 3.23 illustrates an example of a cache coherence problem. As shown in Figure 3.22, the value returned by a given load is not clear because the most recent store may have occurred on a different core. We have to note here that this problem is not very different from the multiprocessor (multiple chips) cache coherence problem. Thus, system designers generally define memory consistency models to specify how a processor core can observe memory accesses from other processor cores in the system.

A multicore system is said to be *cache coherent* if the execution of a given program leads to a valid ordering of reads and writes to a memory location.

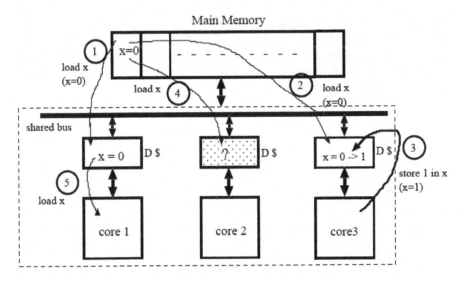

Figure 3.23. *Cache coherence problem example without coherence protocol*

3.4.2. Cache coherence protocols

We have to note first that the solution to the cache coherence problem is a general problem associated with multiprocessors and is only limited to multicore systems or MCSoCs. There exist many coherence algorithms and protocols.

For a small-scale bus-based system, snooping bus is generally used. There are two basic methods to utilize the intercore bus to notify other cores when a core changes something in its cache. One method is referred to as *update*. In the update method, if a core modifies variable "y" it sends the updated value of "y" onto the intercore bus. Each cache always listens (snooping) to the intercore bus so that if a cache sees a variable on the bus which it has a copy of, it will read the updated value. This ensures that all caches have the most up-to-date value of the variable.

Another method that utilizes the intercore bus is called *invalidation*. This method sends an invalidation message onto the intercore bus when a variable is changed. The other caches will read this invalidation signal and if their cores try to access that variable, it will result in a cache miss and the variable will be read from main memory.

The update method causes a significant amount of traffic on the intercore bus because the update signal has to be sent onto the bus every time the variable is updated. However, the invalidation method only requires that an invalidation signal be sent the first time a variable is altered; this is why the invalidation method is the preferred method. Table 3.1 shows all cache coherence states.

State	Permission	Definition
Modified (M)	Read, write	All other caches in I or NP
Exclusive (E)	Read, write	The addressed line is in this cache only
Owned (O)	Read	All other caches in S, I or NP
Shared (S)	Read	All other caches in M or E
Invalid (I)	None	None
Not Present (NP)	None	None

Table 3.1. *Cache coherence states*

Modified, Shared and Invalid (MSI) Protocol: MSI is a basic but well-known cache coherency protocol. These are the three states that a line of cache can be in. The *Modified* state means that a variable in the cache has been modified and therefore has a different value than that found in main memory. The cache is responsible for writing the variable back to main memory. The *Shared* state means that the variable exists in at least one cache and is not modified. The cache can evict the variable without writing it back to the main memory. The *Invalid* state means that the value of the variable has been modified by another cache and this value is invalid.

MESI Protocol: Another well-known cache coherency protocol is the MESI protocol. The Modified and Invalid states are the same for this protocol as they are for the MSI protocol. This protocol introduces a new state – the Exclusive state. The Exclusive state means that the variable is only in this cache and the value of it matches the value within the main memory. This now means that the Shared state indicates that the variable is contained in more than one cache.

Modified, Owned, Shared and Invalid (MOSI) Protocol: The MOSI protocol is identical to the MSI protocol except that it adds an Owned state. The Owned state means that the processor "Owns" the variable and will provide the current value to other caches when requested (or at least it will decide if it will provide it when asked).

The snooping protocol works well with systems based on shared bus (natural broadcast medium). However, large-scale MCSoC (and multiprocessors) may connect cores/processors with memories using switches or some other kind of complex interconnect. Thus, a new method is needed.

The alternative for the "snoopy-bus" scheme is a protocol known as "directory" protocol [CEN 78, CHA 90]. The basic idea in this scheme is to keep track of what is being shared in one centralized place called a directory. This method scales better than snoopy-bus. In this approach, each cache can communicate the state of its variables with a single directory instead of broadcasting the state to all cores.

Cache coherence protocols guarantee that eventually all copies are updated. Depending on how and when these updates are performed, a read operation may sometimes return unexpected values. Consistency deals with which values can be returned to the user by a read operation (may return unexpected values if the update is not complete). The consistency model is a contract that defines what a programmer can expect from the system.

3.5. Conclusion

Increasing processing power demand for new embedded consumer applications made the conventional single-core based designs no longer suitable to satisfy high-performance and low-power consumption demands. In addition, continuous advancements in semiconductor technology enable us to design complex heterogeneous MCSoCs composed of tens or even hundreds of IP cores.

Integrating multiple cores on a single chip has enabled embedded system hardware designers to provide more features and higher processing speeds using less power, thus solving many design problems. However, nothing is really free! The designers of these embedded MCSoCs no longer deal with the familiar homogeneous and symmetric multiprocessing model of large computer systems. Rather, they may have dozens or hundreds of processor cores to program and debug, a heterogeneous and unbalanced mix of DSP, RISC, IPs and complex on-chip network architectures, operating asymmetrically.

3.6. Bibliography

[ALT 12] ALTERA, available at http://www.altera.com/devices/fpga/stratix-fpgas/ stratix-ii/stratixii/features/architecture/st2-lut.html, Accessed January 29, PGAs, 2012.

[BEN 06] BEN ABDALLAH A., SOWA M., "Basic network-on-chip interconnection for future gigascale MCSoCs applications: communication and computation orthogonalization", *Proceedings of Tunisia-Japan Annual Symposium on Society, Science and Technology (TJASSST)*, December 4–9, 2006.

[CEN 78] CENSIER L.M., FEAUTRIER P., "A new solution to coherence problems in multicache systems", *IEEE Transactions on Computers*, vol. C-20, no. 12, pp. 1112–1118, 1978.

[CHA 90] CHAIKEN D., FIELDS C., KURIHARA K. *et al.*, "Directory-based cache coherence in large-scale multiprocessors", *Computer*, vol. 23, no. 6, pp. 49–58, 1990.

[CPO 01] C-PORT CORP., *C-5 Network Processor Architecture Guide*, C-Port Corp., North Andover, 2001.

[ITR 03] ITRS, *International Technology Roadmap for Semiconductors*, System Drivers, 2003.

[ITR 05] ITRS, *International Technology Roadmap for Semiconductors*, System Drivers, 2005.

[KNO 00] KNOBLOCH J., MICCA E., MOTURI M. *et al.*, "A single-chip, 1.6-billion, 16-b MAC/s multiprocessor DSP", *IEEE Journal of Solid-State Circuits*, vol. 35, no. 3, pp. 412–424, 2000.

[PAP 84] PAPAMARCOS M.S., PATEL J.H., "A low-overhead coherence solution for multiprocessors with private cache memories", *Proceedings of the 11th Annual International Symposium on Computer architecture (ISCA)*, pp. 348–354, 1984.

4

Numerical Reproducibility of Parallel and Distributed Stochastic Simulation Using High-Performance Computing

High-performance computing is becoming increasingly important in all scientific disciplines. In this context, accuracy and especially the reproducibility of digital experiments must remain a major concern. The "quest" for reproducibility, essential to any scientific experimentation, is sometimes neglected, especially in parallel stochastic simulations, leading to important implications for the relevance of the results. In this chapter, we propose an analysis of the issues of numerical reproducibility and identify the main obstacles to its implementation. To overcome these obstacles, and propose a set of recommendations relevant for high-performance computing.

4.1. Introduction

Simulation has become an essential tool in many fields of science. It is used to improve our knowledge on complex systems, improve methods and optimize, test and validate the models proposed by scientists. A particularly popular technique is stochastic simulation which includes the Monte Carlo method. These simulations rely on the drawing of pseudo-random numbers. In this class of simulations, the generator of pseudo-random numbers (Pseudo-Random Number Generator [PRNG]) is a fundamental module for

Chapter written by David R.C. HILL. The author would like to thank Van T. Dao, Vincent Breton and Hong Q. Nguyen for their contributions to the chapter.

generating random variables. When the calculations are independent, these simulations are considered easy to parallelize in order to improve their performance with respect to a sequential execution. To rigorously develop a parallel stochastic simulation, it is necessary to have a large number of independent stochastic flows. Such independent flows are achieved by properly generating multiple streams of pseudo-random numbers. Most of these distribution techniques, as well as considerations for the parallelization of PRNGs, are described in [HIL 13] and [LEC 15].

A parallel stochastic simulation is executed on a multiprocessor system. High-performance computing systems are obviously the best choice to improve the execution time. However, the reproducibility of these numerical simulations is even more problematic on high-performance computing systems than on sequential machines. For many simulations, the relevance of the results is questioned [TAU 10, DIE 12, HIL 15].

Research of computer technology enabling resilient numerical reproducibility is becoming increasingly important in the science of computing in general, and especially in stochastic simulation. It is a major criterion for ensuring that a scientist can repeat or remake a published numerical experiment and get the same results. The "reproducibility" therefore has two dimensions: the reproduction of the digital experiment and the exact reproduction of the calculated result (often called numerical reproducibility in the literature).

In this chapter, we present the first results of bibliographic research on numerical reproducibility for parallel stochastic simulations in the context of high-performance computing systems. The three essential contributions of reproducibility are detailed in section 4.2, particularly in the context of parallel stochastic simulations. Section 4.3 describes an analysis of the five major causes of non-reproducibility. Based on these analyses, we propose in section 4.4 four recommendations to improve the reproducibility of experiments and the numerical reproducibility of results obtained by a parallel stochastic simulation.

4.2. Reproducibility and its usefulness for parallel simulation

Let us first deal with some important terminology details. The term "reproducibility" can be too vague and can easily be confusing; it sometimes just means "repeatability" in computer science articles [DRU 09]. Scientific reproducibility aims to reproduce similar results of experiments with possibly different methods and tools. On the other hand, the notion of repeatability means finding exactly the same results when two experiments are conducted with the same input parameters, the same materials and methods within identical contexts.

We also have to pay attention to the term "replication", which is frequently used in English to refer to the concept of repeatability discussed above. But this replication term is widely used in stochastic simulations with another meaning. In the latter context, it is linked in fact to the statistical method enabling us to calculate confidence intervals. The simulation software is then used in identical configurations, with the same input parameters, but with only one change between each replication: the stochastic stream is of course different in producing independent statistical experiments (the result of each replication has to be independent from the others). This is different from the concept of repeatability where "nothing has to change". For repeatability in the IT field, we often use, and somewhat unfairly, the following expression "numerical reproducibility".

Vandewalle and his colleagues proposed a definition of reproducibility being the ability for an independent researcher with the data of an experiment to reproduce the results of the latter [VAN 09]. Long before, Srinivasan [SRI 99] explained that reproducibility for software is the ability to properly obtain the same execution results from one machine to another; this is more often called software portability. Recently, Jimenez found that reproducibility is the ability to run exactly the same simulation and to get the same results [JIM 14]. This is also known as "run to run" reproducibility and actually corresponds to the notions of repeatability or numerical reproducibility.

According to Demmel and Nguyen [DEM 13], numerical reproducibility means obtaining the same results from one run to another including at the bit level (this is known as bitwise reproducibility). In comparison to this definition, Revol and Theveny [REV 14] raise the difficulty of defining the result and its accuracy. They propose an alternative definition of reproducibility, namely to obtain the same result when the scientific computing is executed multiple times, either on the same machine or on different machines, for different numbers of processing units, different execution environments and different workloads. This is the definition that we will retain for this chapter and we call it numerical reproducibility.

From these definitions, we identify three key inputs of numerical reproducibility for parallel stochastic simulations.

INPUT NO. 1.– Numerical reproducibility is used to debug and test a simulation on different runtime environments. If we have the same input data, the same simulation and the same test conditions, then we should get identical results. The verification of this property is up to the author of the simulation.

INPUT NO. 2.– Numerical reproducibility constitutes a method and a standard for judging the appropriateness of a published numerical simulation experiment and its resulting conclusions. The authors of the numerical experiment should answer the following questions:

– do the proposed simulations enable reproducibility?

– how can we reproduce the simulation experiment?

– are the simulation results accurate and credible?

– how do we assess the quality of research results obtained by such computing?

– how can we repeat the results of these simulations?

If we can satisfactorily answer these questions, other scientists can repeat the experiments and find identical results to those presented in the published numerical experiment.

INPUT NO. 3.– Numerical reproducibility is also a way to promote scientific development. In the context of parallel stochastic simulation, numerical reproducibility could mean that the simulation can be repeated with different programming languages using the same standards of scientific computing (including IEEE 754 DEC64 or other standards for scientific calculation), different types of execution (with the ability to compare sequential results to the results obtained with the parallel execution – at small computing scales) and possibly different parallel programming models, etc. This is a very difficult challenge, as soon as the simulation is of complex structure.

4.3. Why do we encounter non-reproducibility?

In the previous section we presented the concept of reproducibility, its variants and its importance in our context of scientific computing with parallel simulations. Proposing a reproducible numerical experiment is not often a simple thing.

According to Jimenez [JIM 14], the result of a computational experiment depends on the system (hardware, the processor cores, the operating system stack, system libraries and configuration), it can also come from the user side (binaries, scripts and 3rd-party libraries) and finally it can also be traced back to input data, parameter values and external services (databases, parallel files system, etc.).

In the case of the parallel stochastic simulation, additional causes must be considered. We classified the causes of non-reproducibility of a simulation into five categories (Figure 4.1): two relate to all types of simulations (scientific publication culture and floating point computing errors) while three have a specific link to parallel stochastic simulations (hardware, software, technical distribution and parallelization) [DAO 14b].

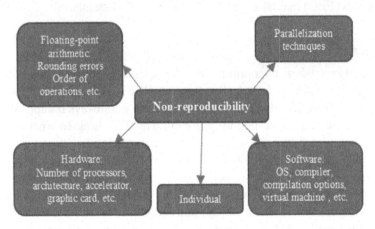

Figure 4.1. *Some reasons for numerical reproducibility failures*

4.3.1. *The scientific publication culture*

Published articles present the results of research but often do not sufficiently specify the practical details, including their research data and source codes. According to a survey by Collberg based on 613 articles in eight ACM conferences, including 515 publications dealing with computational experiments, only 102 publications were reproducible. In this survey, 105 authors were impossible to contact, 179 did not respond to e-mail and 129 recompilation attempts failed [COL 14]. Stodden [STO 10] also studied the consequences of not sharing data and source codes, highlighting the impact of bad habits of the scientific community.

4.3.2. Impact of hardware accelerators

The result of parallel stochastic simulations can be specific to the underlying hardware (hardware accelerators GP-GPUs, FPGAs, Intel Xeon Phi, etc.), thus limiting the portability of scientific applications. When a parallel stochastic simulation runs on several types of equipment, the results are often not identical and we can easily realize that numerical reproducibility is not reached [TAU 10]. The equipment used in the field of high-performance computing is an important source of non-reproducibility. In recent years, we have seen an inflation of the diversity of material causes of non-reproducibility with the introduction of new processors of Floating Point Units (FPU) that no longer meet the IEEE 754 standard.

This is the case of many cores and multicores and mostly of GP-GPU type accelerators. Some discrepancies are still noted between the 32 and 64 bits operations when an optimization for speed is preferred to numerical accuracy. Instruction Level Parallelism (ILP) and code optimization techniques embedded inside microprocessors do not always comply with the order of instructions specified by programmers. This leads to what is known as "Out of Order execution". Most modern processors do propose this feature for speed, but this has an impact on the numerical reproducibility. Diethelm [DIE 12] also studied the impact of a different number of processors on numerical reproducibility. Taufer [TAU 10, TAU 15] indicated that the reproducibility and stability of molecular dynamics simulation results cannot be guaranteed in the case of large-scale parallel simulations performed on GP-GPUs and multicore CPUs. More recently, Corden noted the difficulty and even the impossibility of a bit-wise reproducibility in the family of Intel Xeon Phi accelerators with the k1Om architecture (conventional processors use the "classical" x86 architecture) [COR 13]. The new Intel Xeon Phi (available in 2016/2017) could follow the x86 architecture, but it could also come with ILP features leading to "out of order" executions.

4.3.3. Impact of software

The software contribution to reproducibility problems is related to the implementation of the mathematical library used for accurate calculations, to programming languages, to compilers and their options as well as their associated libraries. We have also observed varying impact depending on the type of virtual machines and the kind of operating systems. In the case of stochastic simulations, the choice of the PRNG, its initialization statuses and the parallelization method used for obtaining independent stochastic flows are specific points of interest for us. Reuillon [REU 08] has shown several limitations to the use of PRNGs for parallel scientific computing. Heinrich had previously detected a list of generators with shortcomings in the CLHEP library such as rand, lrand48, Randu, RNDM, ranmar, ranlux, ranecu and ranarray [HEI 04]. These generators and the library still exist in many scientific applications. Although they might be kept for reproducibility of old software experiments, they are still too often used totally inadequately in modern developments. Similarly, 45 of 58 PRNGs available from the "GNU Scientific Library" have shortcomings in the selection of the initialization pattern [MAT 07]. More recently, we considered non-repeatability of modern PRNGs with respect to the software aspects and we have highlighted several shortcomings linked to portability problems [DAO 14a].

In another context, Glatard [GLA 15] illustrated the problem of non-reproducibility in the analysis of the performance of three software dealing with brain image analysis using different libraries and different interception techniques for system calls. These experiments were done with the gcc compiler and various versions of the C library (glibc) embedded into the executable. This was achieved on Linux operating systems containing the same version of the math library libmath.

4.3.4. Floating point operations

The majority of the simulation results are not numerically reproducible because of the limitations of floating point operations. Indeed, the floating-point representation allows an approximation of a real number on a computer with a mantissa (significand), a base, an exponent and a sign. This is an important type for digital computers found throughout all computing systems [GOL 91]. For high-level programming languages, real numbers are represented by data types in single and double precisions. Each computing system provides standardized math libraries necessary for the floating point computations. Compilers also support floating point types adapted to their respective programming languages. Conventional computers and supercomputers are doing floating point calculations with their arithmetical and logical unit called FPU. The IEEE-754 standard is the most common for a binary representation of floating point arithmetic. This standard is available on almost all modern processors (from AMD and Intel), including the new generation of GPUs dedicated to high-performance computing, the "old" IBM Cell, more modern PowerPC processors and lastly on the latest Intel Xeon Phi family (with "manycores"). All high-performance computing programming languages (Fortran, C and C ++) can enforce compliance with IEEE 754 (32 and 64 bits). By default, some languages use the 10 bytes available in modern FPU for precision calculations (with 80 bits), but they often ignore the correct rounding properties of the IEEE 754 standard. This has very significant impacts on results. Between 1998 and 2004, conferences from Dahan and Darcy (Berkeley and Stanford) reported problems of this type, with particular problems for the Java language. One of the most famous conferences was precisely named: "How Java Floating Point hurts everyone everywhere" (https://www.cs.berkeley.edu/~wkahan/JAVAhurt. pdf). In the latest version of the IEEE 754 standard proposed in 2008, the limitations clearly identified the associativity problem (the impact of the order of operations) and the management of rounding errors in addition and multiplications. Limitations were again clearly demonstrated to all the scientific community. Many studies indicate these limitations in a reproducibility context [DEM 13, REV 14] and recall the often overlooked fundamentals which Goldberg taught since [GOL 91].

4.3.5. *Technique to distribute random parallel streams*

For rigorous parallel stochastic computing, one must have "independent" stochastic streams, as many as needed by the parallel application. If improperly performed, the parallelization of a stochastic application is also a source of non-reproducibility. The different order of execution within a set of threads in parallel, the "parallelization" of a PRNG, as well as the assignment of different independent streams to the processors may impact the results. Hellekalek showed the potential risk of "correlation" in the distribution methods of different stochastic flows to different processors. The title of one of his articles at the IEEE/ACM PADS Conference in 1998 is "Do not trust parallel Monte Carlo" [HEL 98]. This warning is still relevant in 2016. More recently, the Taufer's team [TAU 15] showed the impact of the assignment of floating point calculations to threads with a different order of execution of threads, related to rounding error and lack of associativity of the calculation in floating point. In addition, the number of threads, the number of pseudo-random numbers flows and the number of calculations per flow can affect the accuracy of results. This source of numerical non-reproducibility impacts comparisons between sequential and parallel executions or between parallel executions. A state of the art of correct techniques is proposed in [HIL 13] as well as a design method to obtain numerically reproducible results for parallel stochastic simulations, with a comparison between the results obtained by the sequential and parallel version of a simulation code.

4.4. Some recommendations

In order to completely reproduce a stochastic parallel simulation using a high-performance computing system, we must ensure the repeatability of the experiment and its numerical reproducibility. We should be able to exactly repeat the numerical experience published by the author. If the authors share their "scientific data", including their source code, their input parameters and their raw data, such repeatability can really be considered. In order to achieve this goal, we propose a set of recommendations.

RECOMMENDATION 1.– To be able to repeat a parallel stochastic simulation experiment, with the availability of similar hardware equipment, we need the author's scientific data. These data broadly consist of:

– the source code of the final version that was used to generate the published results;

– the data used (if any);

– the set of input parameters;

– additional scripts (if any);

– information on the resources used (hardware, number of processors, software, operating system, compiler, programming library, virtual machine, additional packages);

– a guide explaining, step by step, the start of the launching of the numerical experiment, the description of this experiment, the history of major bug fixes and version of the code;

– constraints and dependencies associated with the computer technology used and data processing records (the calculation tool, the data tables obtained, tools to create images or graphics if any);

– the simulation model (implemented in sequential and/or parallel) and the inputs and outputs of the model of the class structure if any (algorithms, etc.);

– a description of the tackled simulation problem.

These data are required for a reproducible scientific publication. In other words, the reproducibility of numerical experiments should allow a scientist in the domain to download all data available online, as well as information and complete documents concerning the computational experience. In the current state of research in computer science, this involves a change in the culture of communication of scientific results.

Before the distribution of scientific data and information, authors should apply a reproducible standard research norm – such as Reproducible Research Standard, (RRS) [STO 09] – not only to ensure their ownership but mainly to facilitate numerical reproducibility, reuse and redistribution by colleagues. RRS not only includes software, but also the procedures and the description of the hardware required for the replication of computational experiments. It also ensures that this is done without fault by peers. Indeed, it has additional tools such as the online sharing of scientific data with Web sites similar to github.com, bitbucket.org, RunMyCode.org and sodata.org (or other similar sites). RSS also advocates the replication of an experiment with tools such as CDE or ReproZip [STO 13].

After being able to rerun a numerical experience, if we get the same results as the author, the published results are considered significantly more reliable.

RECOMMENDATION 2.– This recommendation focuses on the techniques needed to accurately reproduce the results of a stochastic simulation. This recommendation applies to authors who must always think about the quality of their scientific work when developing simulations.

The points to watch for are the following:

– the choice of good libraries offering an implementation of mathematical data types following the IEEE standard for single and double precision of floating points [ROB 13];

– a careful attention to the order of execution of floating point calculations;

– the use of techniques to increase the reproducibility summation in floating point such as that proposed by Kahn with composite precision [TAU 15];

– the use of the best PRNGs;

– the use of the proper initialization methods for the PRNGs (for sequential and parallel applications PRAND, clRNG, SPRNG, etc.) [LEC 15];

– a rigorous assignment of stochastic streams to the computing elements [HIL 15, LEC 16];

– the program has to be designed by thinking parallel even in the sequential version to be able to compare the final results with a parallelized version [HIL 15].

RECOMMENDATION 3.– We must be careful about the execution environment of a simulation before the publication of results. When possible, running the application on at least two different runtime environments is important to assess the impact of:

– the difference in hardware (GP-GPUs, MPPA, Xeon Phi Manycore, etc.);

– the difference between compilers and compiler versions;

– the difference between operating systems and virtual machines;

– the different number of cores from one execution to the other;

– compiler options that improve numerical reproducibility. For instance, with an Intel processor and compiler, using standard settings leads to non-reproducible results. If accuracy is more important than computing speed, the use of compiler options such as "-fp-model precise", "-fp-model source" and "-fp-no-fma" allows, for example, to repeat the results from one execution to another. Such options reduce the difference between the results obtained on different Intel architectures. For example, we can obtain very similar results even when using classical Intel Xeon multicores and Xeon Phi many cores, which do not have exactly the same architecture (x86 vs. k10m); the latter architecture does not, by the way, guarantee a bitwise reproducibility [DAO 14b].

RECOMMENDATION 4.– Avoid using too many specific hardware resources for numerical repeatability.

Should the development of a parallel application require specific hardware, repeatability will not be reached in a different environment. At least, if numerical reproducibility cannot be met, scientific reproducibility can still be reached with respect to the corroboration aspects introduced previously. This can lead to:

– the use of different hardware and different software from one experiment to the other;

– the comparison of results obtained by different sequential and parallel implementations;

– the use of different programming models;

– the use of different programming languages.

All these recommendations enable progress on a difficult path. It is still possible to develop reproducible software, but we are still far from a method applicable to all contexts.

4.5. Conclusion

This chapter offers a review of the state of the art of numerical reproducibility with a particular focus on parallel stochastic simulations. This article also aims to increase the sensitivity of the scientific community to the need for numerical reproducibility in the field of simulation; this will increase the quality of publications and help save time spent trying to reproduce a bad numerical simulation (with the financial investment that accompanies it).

We have found five main causes of numerical non-reproducibility and identified three key inputs of numerical reproducibility for the simulation field. Besides a presentation of all the major problems that can lead to failures in terms of numerical reproducibility, we have proposed a set of recommendations. The first suggests a change in our scientific publication culture in terms of computational experiments. The second recommendation proposes a technique to design a reproducible application. The third recommendation suggests testing our application on at least two different execution environments and if necessary to develop a truly reproducible new release. The fourth recommendation addresses issues of improvements to corroborate the results of simulations in the absence of numerical reproducibility, especially in the case of hybrid computing where we are mixing different hardware architectures or different parallel programming models. For a numerical reproducibility of computational experiments, it will always be necessary to have all the data and information for the considered experiment.

This work on reproducibly is mainly supported by the University Agency of "Francophonie" and the International Institute "Francophonie".

4.6. Bibliography

[COL 14] COLLBERG C., PROEBSTING T., MORAILA G., et al., "Measuring reproducibility in computer systems research", Technical report, available at http://reproducibility.cs.arizona.edu/tr.pdf, 2014.

[COR 13] CORDEN M., "Run-to-run reproducibility of floating-point calculations for applications on Intel Xeon Phi coprocessors (and Intel Xeon Processors)", Available at https://software.intel.com/en-us/articles/run-to-run-reproducibility-of-floating-point-calculations-for-applications-on-intel-xeon, 2013.

[DAO 14a] DAO V.T., MAIGNE L., MAZEL C. et al., "Numerical reproducibility, portability and performance of modern pseudo random number generators: preliminary study for parallel stochastic using hybrid Xeon Phi computing processors", *Proceedings of the 28th European Simulation and Modeling, ESM'2014*, pp. 80–87, October 2014.

[DAO 14b] DAO V.T., BRETON V., NGUYEN H.Q. *et al.*, "Numerical reproducibility for high performance computing: The case of parallel stochastic simulations", *Proceedings of the 9th International Student Conference on Advanced Science and Technology, ICAST'2014*, pp. 139–140, December 2014.

[DEM 13] DEMMEL J., NGUYEN H.D., "Numerical reproducibility and accuracy at exascale", *IEEE Symposium on Computer Arithmetic (ARITH)*, pp. 235–237, 2013.

[DIE 12] DIETHELM K., "The limits of reproducibility in numerical simulation", *Computing in Science and Engineering*, vol. 14, no. 1, pp. 64–72, 2012.

[DRU 09] DRUMOND C., "Replicability is not reproducibility: nor is it good science", *Proceedings of the Evaluation Methods for Machine Learning Workshop, 26th International Conference for Machine Learning*, Montreal, Canada, 2009.

[GLA 15] GLATARD T., LEWIS L.B., FERREIRA DA SILVA R. *et al.*, "Reproducibility of neuroimaging analyses across operating systems", *Frontiers in Neuroinformatics*, vol. 9, pp. 1–12, 2015.

[GOL 91] GOLDBERG D., "What every computer scientist should know about floating-point arithmetic", *ACM Computing Surveys*, vol. 23, no. 1, pp. 5–48, 1991.

[HEI 04] HEINRICH J., "Detecting a bad random number generator", Available at http://www-cdf.fnal.gov/physics/statistics/notes/cdf6850_badrand.pdf, January 2004.

[HEL 98] HELLEKALEK P., "Don't trust parallel Monte Carlo!", *Proceedings of the 12th Workshop on Parallel and Distributed Simulation (PADS'98)*, pp. 82–89, 1998.

[HIL 13] HILL D.R.C., PASSERAT-PALMBACH J., MAZEL C. *et al.*, "Distribution of random streams for simulation practitioners", *Concurrency and Computation: Practice and Experience, Special Issue*, vol. 25, no. 10, pp. 1427–1442, 2013.

[HIL 15] HILL D.R.C., "Parallel random numbers, simulation, science and reproducibility", *IEEE/AIP – Computing in Science and Engineering*, vol. 17, no. 4, pp. 66–71, 2015.

[JIM 14] JIMENEZ I., MALTZAHN C., MOODY A., "Redo: reproducibility at scale", Technical report, UCSC-SOE-14-12, available at https://www.soe.ucsc.edu/research/technical-reports/UCSC-SOE-14-12, 2014.

[LEC 16] L'ECUYER P., Munger D., ORESHKIN B. *et al.*, "Random numbers for parallel computers: requirements and methods, with emphasis on GPUs", *Mathematics and Computers in Simulation*, http://dx.doi.org/10.1016/j.matcom.2016.05.0050378-4754/, 2016.

[MAT 07] MATSUMOTO M., WADA I., KURAMOTO A. *et al.*, "Common defects in initialization of pseudo random number generators", *ACM Transactions on Modeling and Computer Simulation (TOMACS)*, available at: http://dx.doi.org/ 10.1145/1276927.1276928, vol. 17, no. 4, 2007.

[REU 08] REUILLON R., Simulations stochastiques en environnements distribués: Application aux grille de calcul, PhD Thesis, Blaise Pascal University, 2008.

[REV 14] REVOL N., THÉVENY P., "Numerical reproducibility and parallel computations: Issues for interval algorithms", *IEEE Transactions on Computer*, vol. 63, no. 8, pp. 1915–1924, 2014.

[ROB 13] ROBEY R.W., "Reproducibility for parallel programming", *Bit-wise reproducibility Workshop at SC13*, LA-UR-13-24380, available at https://github. com/losalamos/Exascale_Docs/blob/master/Reproducibility.pdf, November 22, 2013.

[SRI 99] SRINIVASAN A., CEPERLEY D.M., MASCAGNI M., "Random number generators for parallel applications", in PRIGOGINE I., RICE S.A. (eds), *Advances in Chemical Physics: Monte Carlo Methods in Chemical Physics*, John Wiley & Sons, Inc., Hoboken, USA, vol. 105, pp. 13–35, 1999.

[STO 09] STODDEN V., "The reproducible research standard: reducing legal barriers to scientific knowledge and innovation", *IEEE Computing in Science & Engineering*, vol. 11, no. 1, pp. 35–40, 2009.

[STO 10] STODDEN V., "The scientific method in practice: reproducibility in the computational sciences", *MIT Sloan Research*, Paper No. 4773-10, 2010.

[STO 13] STODDEN V., BAILEY D.H., BORWEIN J., *et al.*, "Setting the default to reproducible: reproducibility in computational and experimental mathematics", ICERM Workshop Report, 2013.

[TAU 10] TAUFER M., PARDON O., SAPONARO P. *et al.*, "Improving numerical reproducibility and stability in large-scale numerical simulations on GPUs", *IEEE Symposium on Parallel and Distributed Processing*, pp. 1–9, 2010.

[TAU 15] TAUFER M., BECCHI M., JOHNSTON T. *et al.*, "Numerical reproducibility challenges on extreme scale multi-threading GPUs", *NVIDIA GPU Technology Conference*, San Jose, available at http://ondemand.gputechconf. com/gtc/2015/ presentation/Michela-Taufer.pdf, 2015.

[VAN 09] VANDEWALLE P., KOVACEVIC J., VETTERLI M., "Reproducible research in signal processing - what, why, and how", *IEEE Signal Processing Magazine*, vol. 26, no. 3, pp. 37–47, 2009.

List of Authors

Abderazak BEN ABDALLAH
University of Aizu
Aizuwakamatsu
Japan

David R.C. HILL
University Clermont Auvergne
Clermont Ferrand
France

Andreas TOLK
MITRE Corporation
Hampton
USA

Mamadou Kaba TRAORÉ
University Clermont Auvergne
Clermont Ferrand
France

Bernard P. ZEIGLER
University of Arizona
Tucson
USA

Index

Printed in the United States
By Bookmasters